KNITTING

KNITTING

TREASURE PRESS

First published in Great Britain in 1984 by
Octopus Books Limited

This edition published in 1986 by
Treasure Press
59 Grosvenor Street
London W1

© 1984 Octopus Books Limited

ISBN 1 85051 133 0

Printed in Hong Kong

CONTENTS

HISTORY

Knitting today is one of the most widely practised crafts, but this has not always been the case. The origins of hand-knitting are very obscure and it is difficult to trace the development of the craft.

The earliest evidence of knitted garments indicates that ancient Arabia was probably the birthplace of knitting. Some of the oldest remnants known are shaped woollen socks which date from as early as the second and third centuries. These early knitters were nomadic tribesmen, who, with their flocks and families, travelled vast distances over the Arab sub-continent. The herds supplied the fleece which the women spun into yarn, to be knitted by the men while tending the sheep. The earliest garments would have been fairly simple and practical, such as robes, socks and caps. But with the Arabs' love of coloured things, their knitting became intricately patterned and coloured from the seventh century onwards. It is quite easy to find links between this early work and the exquisite Florentine and Spanish knitted silk garments of the period between the twelfth and sixteenth centuries. Their influence can also be seen in the designs on Fair Isle sweaters. One of the oldest surviving knitted garments is a stocking from the late eleventh or early twelfth century, which was excavated in Egypt, but thought to have origins further to the East.

The art of knitting was probably introduced to Europe by the Coptic monks and missionaries of Egypt who travelled far and wide in the known world. In Egypt 'Coptic caps' are known to have been worn by these men as early as 1000 to 1200 A.D. Their influence spread to Europe with the invasion of the Moors into Spain. Medieval garments were discovered in the tombs of the royal family of Castile dating from the thirteenth century. They were decorated with superb motifs in stranded knitting of groups of birds, fleur-de-lis, eight-pointed stars and geometric designs. But it was not until the fourteenth and fifteenth centuries that the first written records to have survived were produced.

The Middle Ages saw the spread of knitting through the rest of Europe, with Spain remaining the home of hand-knitted silken

◁ *Twentieth-century Spanish gloves knitted in red silk and gilt yarns.*

▷ *Two-toed socks worked in red three-ply wool, from fourth-century Egypt.*

▷ *A section of an exquisite example of Shetland lace, a cape made in the Shetland Islands in the nineteenth century.*

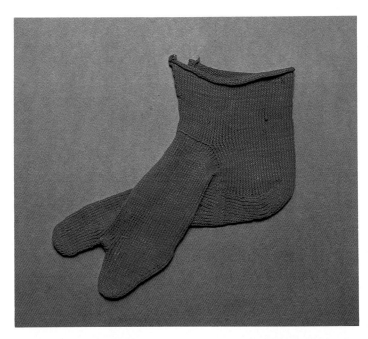

hosiery. As in France and Italy, the Church played a major role in the development of the craft. It gave its patronage to the newly formed Knitting Guilds and used vestments and furnishings worked from the finest quality knitwear.

Throughout Europe the Guilds were strictly controlled for members and apprentices wishing to become Master Knitters. Membership was restricted to male knitters, the only women members being widows who took the place of their husbands. A boy wishing to join the Guild was apprenticed to a Master for three years in his workshop to learn the rudiments of the trade, and then a further three years were spent travelling abroad to experience different knitting traditions. At the end of this period he had to pass rigorous examinations by producing several intricately patterned pieces in a short space of time, before he qualified as a Master Knitter. The work of these craftsmen was of such high quality that it was generally only afforded by royalty or persons within the royal courts.

The Tudor and Elizabethan period (1485-1603) saw England become the leader of the knitting industry throughout the world. The standard of Guild craftsmanship was very high, and the basics of knitting spread quickly amongst the poorer people enabling them to fashion simple garments from knitted felting. Gradually hand-knitting spread throughout the country as a main village craft, and was particularly important in those areas where sheep farming

knitting survived as a flourishing and productive craft.

The latter part of the seventeenth century saw the collapse of the hosiery industry in the Channel Islands, due to scarcity of supplies of fine yarn and the introduction of mechanized knitting. The inherent knitting skills of the male population of these islands were adapted to the demands of the developing fishing industry, and they were quick to use their knowledge of knitting to produce 'gansey' sweaters. These garments were practical rather than decorative and were knitted in handspun navy four- or five-ply yarn. The 'oiled' nature of the yarn made them weatherproof. For centuries guernseys or 'ganseys' took one of two forms. The everyday plain sweater worked in stocking stitch, or the ones worn on special occasions which were decorated with intricate patterns. A guernsey was worked in the round with each village having its own distinctive design, which was handed down from generation to generation by word of mouth. Gradually the isolation of these areas disappeared and the patterns became less distinctive. The knitting of these traditional 'ganseys' declined further with the declining importance of the coastal fishing communities, the use of thicker yarns, and less complicated printed patterns.

The remote Aran Islands have, historically, been another centre of knitting. Their position on one of the main trading routes of Europe made contact between Ireland and the Mediterranean countries, such as Spain and Egypt, a possibility. Travelling monks and missionaries were probably responsible for the introduction of the craft to Aran. The inspiration for the very distinctive form of Aran knitwear came from the everyday working life and local surroundings. Great use was, and still is, made of bobbles, cables and crossed stitches, which reflect such things as rocky landscapes, fishermen's ropes, and the importance of religion to the islanders. This unique style of knitting is still in as much demand as it ever was.

Fair Isle, one of the Shetland Islands, gave its name to another style of distinctive patterned knitwear. The Shetland Islands have also seen many sea travellers from distant lands, from the early Viking raiders to the later traders of the Mediterranean. Shipwrecked sailors from the Armada may have been responsible for the introduction of coloured knitting, in the Spanish style, to the people of Fair Isle. Since the sixteenth century, knitted work has been the main source of trade with the mainland. Traditional Fair Isle sweaters were knitted in the round with intricate all-over patterns, using wool spun from the local sheep. The natural vegetable dyes taken from the surrounding landscape of the island gave them a unique appearance. Fair Isle knitwear has always been popular and became even more so after the Prince of Wales, later Edward VIII, was photographed in the 1920s wearing one while playing golf.

During the latter half of the eighteenth century, amateur knitters in the Shetland Islands developed a form of lace knitting, which was made on extremely thin steel needles using the fine soft wool taken from around the sheep's neck. The inspiration for this work came from an exhibition of fine Spanish lace which was brought to the Islands earlier in the century. Several examples of this intricate work still survive. Some of these are the Shetland shawls, from the most northerly island of Unst, which are among the finest examples of lace knitting. Traditionally they were made for christenings or as wedding veils. They were fine enough to slip through a wedding ring, and are fashioned from only ten basic stitch patterns. Today it is a dying art and very few knitters capable of this exquisite work remain on the islands.

During the first half of the nineteenth century hand-knitting remained in a very depressed state. Some encouragement was given with the introduction of printed women's journals for ladies of the better social classes with spare time to fill. They were prompted to knit socks for the troops during the Crimean War and garments for the poor.

The late nineteenth century saw hand-knitting being taken-up again as a fashionable amateur pastime. Like sketching and music, it

was another source of income, such as the Yorkshire dales, where the finest wools were produced. In England also, the religious influence in the knitting industry during the sixteenth and seventeenth centuries was very important, with some of the finest silk knitting being done in the monasteries and nunneries.

Queen Elizabeth I encouraged the knitting industry in Jersey and Guernsey by establishing local guilds to promote the industry in order to guarantee the supply of finely knitted hosiery for the English courts, and also to discourage the male population of the islands from continuing with their main source of income – smuggling. By the seventeenth century, with this encouragement, knitting for export to England became the main industry of the islands.

The Guilds remained active in Europe until the eighteenth century, when large-scale use of knitting frames made hand-knitting uneconomical for commercial purposes. In England, Queen Elizabeth had refused to grant a patent to William Lee, the inventor of the knitting frame for stockings, as she believed that it would take away from poor people their only source of income.

Eventually the adaptation of the knitting frame, as part of the greater movement of the Industrial Revolution at the end of the eighteenth century, led to the demise of the hand-knitting industry. It survived only in the more isolated parts of England, such as the Yorkshire dales, Scotland, the Channel Islands, the Aran Islands and Fair Isle, where mechanisation was slow to encroach. It was in those areas where the isolation forced a closer financial dependence on local industries, such as sheep farming and fishing, that hand-was thought to be a desirable accomplishment for the well-educated lady of the day. Experimentation with combinations of stitches and yarns was encouraged by the Victorians' love of ornamentation and decoration.

By World War I the popularity of hand-knitting had again declined dramatically, and with the enormous influx and availability of cheap, mass-produced, machine knitted garments, the craft receded further into the background. The range of yarns and patterns became very limited, and the craft survived only on a very basic level for many years.

During the last decade, with the increased interest being shown in the arts and crafts industry, hand-knitting has seen a great revival of interest. New and exciting yarns have appeared on the market to inspire knitters. Young fashion designers are seeing the craft as a new area for creative expression, and developing many unusual designs. There is an enormous wealth of knitting traditions to draw upon and a great many innovative techniques are being employed. One of the strongest trends in recent years has been towards the use of unconventional materials in knitting. These have included anything from strips of leather to plastic sheeting cut into strips, narrow satin ribbon, shoelaces, rags and even Christmas tinsel. In such cases, the texture of the knitted fabric becomes more important than intricate stitch patterns and complicated garment shapes or colour patterns. Many of the new yarns being produced are both multicoloured and multitextured and are an interesting commercial reflection of this new style. Knitting today can be viewed as an expanding craft where the only limit to its variety is the knitter's imagination.

◁ *The Duke of Windsor, playing golf at Biarritz and wearing the Fair Isle pullover which he was to make famous.*

▷ *Turn-of-the-century Cornish fisherman wearing a local 'gansey'.*

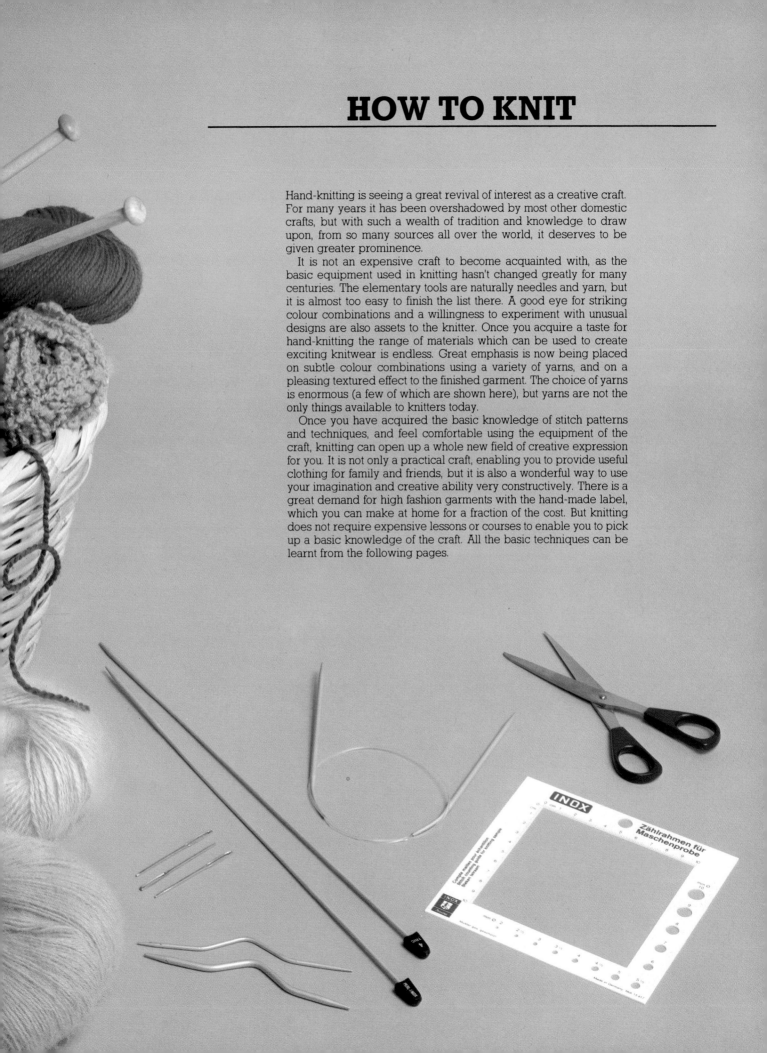

HOW TO KNIT

Hand-knitting is seeing a great revival of interest as a creative craft. For many years it has been overshadowed by most other domestic crafts, but with such a wealth of tradition and knowledge to draw upon, from so many sources all over the world, it deserves to be given greater prominence.

It is not an expensive craft to become acquainted with, as the basic equipment used in knitting hasn't changed greatly for many centuries. The elementary tools are naturally needles and yarn, but it is almost too easy to finish the list there. A good eye for striking colour combinations and a willingness to experiment with unusual designs are also assets to the knitter. Once you acquire a taste for hand-knitting the range of materials which can be used to create exciting knitwear is endless. Great emphasis is now being placed on subtle colour combinations using a variety of yarns, and on a pleasing textured effect to the finished garment. The choice of yarns is enormous (a few of which are shown here), but yarns are not the only things available to knitters today.

Once you have acquired the basic knowledge of stitch patterns and techniques, and feel comfortable using the equipment of the craft, knitting can open up a whole new field of creative expression for you. It is not only a practical craft, enabling you to provide useful clothing for family and friends, but it is also a wonderful way to use your imagination and creative ability very constructively. There is a great demand for high fashion garments with the hand-made label, which you can make at home for a fraction of the cost. But knitting does not require expensive lessons or courses to enable you to pick up a basic knowledge of the craft. All the basic techniques can be learnt from the following pages.

Materials and equipment

YARNS

The selection of yarns available has never been so wide as it is today. They include animal, plant and man-made fibres, and any combination in between.

Yarns are sold commercially in different plies; a ply being a single strand of thread. It does not indicate the exact thickness of the yarn, as each single thread is not a definite thickness. Classic yarns are combinations of the same threads spun together into different plies, whilst newer style yarns, such as bouclé, lurex or chenille, are combinations of different threads spun together to give various textured effects. The individual nature of each yarn is achieved by varying the method in which these plies are twisted together into a workable yarn. A soft yarn is produced by loose twisting, and a tighter twist makes a yarn more hard-wearing. Natural yarns may be more gentle to the touch, but require more care than synthetic yarns. They are generally more expensive than synthetics as well. In England yarn is sold in balls, by metric weight, not length, which is carefully controlled by a British standards regulation. Below is a description of the most commonly used yarns available today.

Sheep's wool is the most versatile of all fibres. It gives unrivalled warmth, comfort, strength and durability, as well as excellent insulation against cold weather. The finest wool comes from Merino sheep, bred in Australia, and is usually sold commercially under the name of 'Botany Wool'. It can be used in nearly any knitted garment but with due regard given to the need for careful hand-washing.

Cashmere wool is produced from the cashmere goat from the north-easterly areas of Tibet. Originally, the name came from the province in India where fine cashmere shawls have been made for centuries, Kashmir. Only the softest fleece from the undercoat and the beard of the goat is used for this yarn, and it has always been considered a luxury yarn. It is very fine and silky, extremely warm and lightweight, and can be dyed well in any subtle shade.

Mohair wool is enjoying a great revival of popularity, and is used widely in combination with other yarns. It comes from the coat of the angora goat, and has a luxurious feel and sheen, and is easily and successfully dyed.

Angora wool is the extremely light and fluffy wool taken from the angora rabbits which are bred in France. It is a relatively new yarn, having only been developed during this century. Because of its extreme fluffiness it is usually spun together with other wool which then produces excellent insulating properties. If used alone it breaks easily and is not very hard-wearing.

Alpaca wool comes from the South American llama. They prefer the high altitude countries along the Pacific Coast, such as Peru and Chile, but there are strict controls on the amount of wool able to be exported from these countries. Because of the shortage of supply it is usually spun together with other wool, and makes an excellent yarn for hand-knitting. It is lustrous and soft to the touch, but has hard-wearing and resilient properties as well.

Shetland wool is a traditional yarn from the Shetland sheep, dyed in natural soft colours and knitted into warm, hard-wearing garments such as vests, sweaters, mittens, gloves and scarves.

Aran wool is a thick, natural and unbleached yarn used in traditional Aran knitting for making excellent outdoor garments such as sweaters and jackets. It offers great warmth and weather resistance.

Brushed yarns have become very popular with hand-knitters in recent years. They are usually spun with some mohair or long-haired angora, in combination with other yarns. The hairs are brushed out during the spinning process to give the softness. They are very warm and easily cared for, as many of them are specially

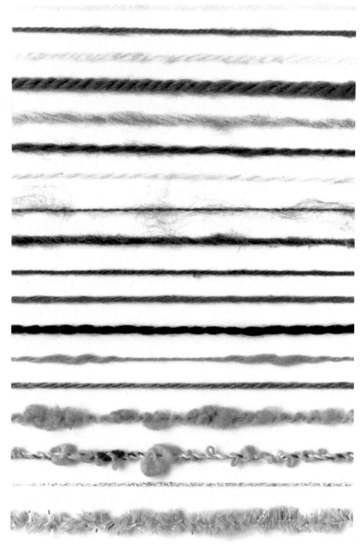

Key to picture on pages 10-11: 1 tape measure; 2 double-pointed needles; 3 stitch holders; 4 large wooden knitting needles; 5 metal or plastic-coated knitting needles; 6 wool sewing needles; 7 cable needles; 8 circular needle; 9 scissors; 10 needle gauge.

treated so as to be safely machine washable.

Synthetic yarns include orlon, nylon, rayon and dralon threads, usually spun together with a small amount of fine woollen yarn. Unmixed they pick up a great deal of static electricity, but are easily machine washed and dried. This has made them extremely popular for use in babies' and children's garments.

Silk comes from the labours of the silk worm, and is another extremely luxurious yarn. It offers high lustre, strength and softness, elasticity and resilience, but needs great care in washing and ironing.

Cotton is the most widely used vegetable fibre and has quite different properties to that of wool. It lacks elasticity, but knits easily and well. Being a natural fibre it is hard-wearing and can be dyed to any colour with no difficulty. It is cool to wear and is excellent when made into summer garments, and washes and irons well.

Lurex yarns are manufactured from thin strips of plastic-coated aluminium. The plastic can be different colours and is usually combined with rayon to produce brightly coloured, shiny yarns, but when spun together with other yarns gives a broken glitter effect in the knitting.

But with so much emphasis on texture in today's hand-knitting, it is not necessary to confine oneself to knitting with only traditional yarns. Using a little imagination it is quite easy to incorporate such materials as leather or suede strips, lengths of plastic, ribbon or braid, shoelaces, tinsel or string, to give an exciting texture.

KNITTING NEEDLES

These are the principal tools of the craft of hand-knitting. They are sold in pairs and a wide variety of sizes. Gradually all are being converted to metric sizing, and the numbers are indicated on the knob end of each needle. In metric sizes the larger the number shown, the larger the needle. They are generally made of plastic or coated metal, but in the very large sizes, used for chunky yarns, they may also be found in wood.

The size of the needles varies with the thickness of the yarn and the finished effect that the knitter desires. The smaller the needle, the tighter the knitting, and the larger the needle the looser is the work. When experimenting with your own designs it is not necessary to confine yourself to the size of needle traditionally used for the chosen yarn, as exciting textures can be created by deviating from the recommended sizes.

Needles are also sold in different lengths, and the choice should be made according to whichever length feels the most comfortable for the knitter. They should be carefully stored in a dry, clean place so they do not become bent. Straight, clean needles facilitate even and fast knitting.

Circular needles are made with pointed plastic or coated metal sections on both ends of a flexible nylon section. They are also sold in different lengths and sizes, but care must be taken when deciding to use them so that the number of stitches easily reaches between the two pointed ends. They are simpler to use than sets of four needles, and a whole garment can be knitted on them, without seams to the armholes, especially when working plain knitting over a large number of stitches.

Double-pointed needles have points at both ends and are used usually in sets of four to knit circular items in the round, such as socks and sometimes neckbands.

Wool needles are specifically designed for the sewing together of knitted garments. They have a large eye at one end for ease of threading yarns, and a blunt end to avoid splitting the yarn in the knitted pieces.

Stitch holders are generally used in the shaping of necklines. When it is necessary to reserve some stitches from the body or the sleeves of the work, they are placed on a stitch holder until knitted into the main garment.

Needle gauges are usually plastic or metal frames with graduated holes which indicate the correct size of knitting needles.

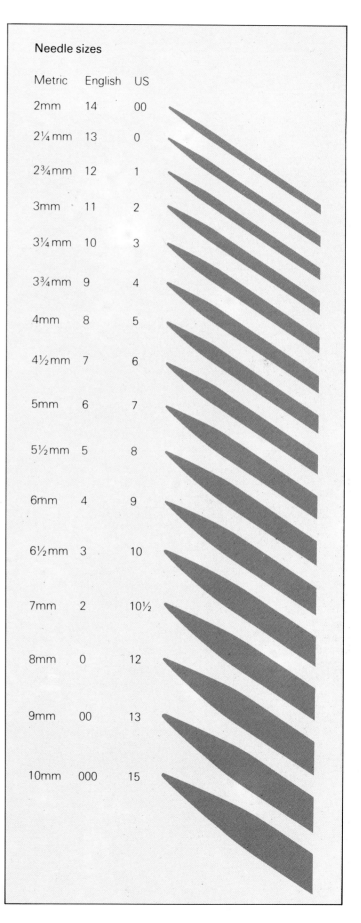

Needle sizes		
Metric	English	US
2mm	14	00
2¼mm	13	0
2¾mm	12	1
3mm	11	2
3¼mm	10	3
3¾mm	9	4
4mm	8	5
4½mm	7	6
5mm	6	7
5½mm	5	8
6mm	4	9
6½mm	3	10
7mm	2	10½
8mm	0	12
9mm	00	13
10mm	000	15

Basic skills

Before attempting to knit any garment, it is necessary to master a few basic knitting techniques and stitches. It is advisable to practise with any scraps of yarn so as to feel confident when tackling a pattern, and to feel comfortable using the correct equipment.

The basics of learning to knit are very simple – casting-on, casting-off, increasing and decreasing, and the two elementary stitches of knit and purl. Most patterns consist of differing combinations of these two stitches.

The most common method of casting-on and casting-off is the two-needle method. Casting-off may be done on a knit or a purl row, or even across a ribbed band. The method required will be indicated in the pattern being used.

1. Make a single loop leaving a short length of yarn for finishing off, and place it on the left-hand needle. Hold the loose end firmly, put the right-hand needle to the left of the initial loop. Pass the yarn under and over the point of the needle, from left to right.

2. Draw the loop on the right-hand needle through to the front of the work, and place it firmly on the left-hand needle.

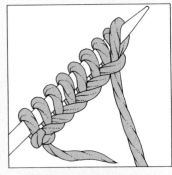

3. Place the right-hand needle between the first two stitches, pass yarn under and over as before, draw yarn through and put it on the left-hand needle.

4. Continue making stitches in this way until the correct number has been cast-on to the left-hand needle.

The knit stitch

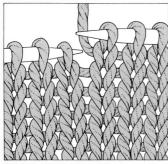 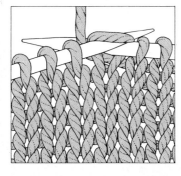 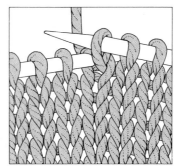

1. Hold the needle with the stitches to be knitted in the left hand with the yarn at the back of the work.

2. Put the right-hand needle through the first stitch, take the yarn under and over the end of the right-hand needle.

3. Pull the new loop on the right-hand needle through the work to the front and slip original stitch off the left-hand needle.

Beginning a new row
Arriving at the end of the first row all the stitches should be on the right-hand needle. Transfer this needle to the left hand ready to commence the second row.

The purl stitch

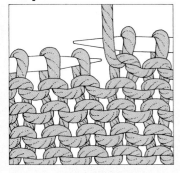 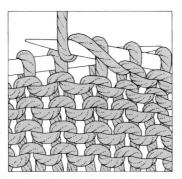 

1. Hold the stitches to be purled in the left hand with the yarn at the front of the work.

2. Put the right-hand needle through the front of the first stitch, pass the yarn over and around right-hand needle from right to left.

3. Pull the new loop through the stitch and slip it from the left-hand needle, and so the new stitch will remain on the right-hand needle.

Changing from knit to purl

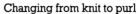
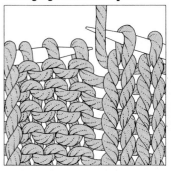

After completing the knit stitch bring the yarn through to the front of the work between the needles. Purl the next stitch in the usual way.

Far left is a photograph of stocking stitch as viewed from the front of the work. One row is plain and the next is purled and this combination is continued. The right side is smooth and the back is ridged as in the second photograph. When this side of stocking stitch is used as the right side of the work, it is known as reverse stocking stitch. When every row is knitted or every row is purled the stitch is known as garter stitch.

JOINING YARN

It is best to try not to run out of yarn in the middle of a row, as the joining knot will be evident from the front of the work. If it is unavoidable, use the following method to join the yarn. Unravel short ends of the two pieces of yarn, and overlap half the strands from each piece. Twist them together firmly. Cut the remaining threads. This method is known as 'splicing' the yarn.

PICKING UP DROPPED STITCHES

When a dropped stitch occurs a little patience will overcome the problem. It is not necessary to pull out the needle and undo several rows. Picking up is easily done on a simple stitch pattern, but much more difficult in the course of a complicated pattern. When it occurs in a pattern, and after you have rectified the problem, always check that the number of stitches is correct before continuing with the work. To pick up a dropped stitch the only equipment you need to use is a crochet hook.

Picking up a knit stitch

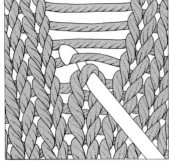

With the right side facing put the hook into the back of the dropped stitch. Place the hook around the thread immediately above the dropped stitch and pull the thread through the stitch. Do this until the same level is reached as the rest of the work and place the stitch on the left-hand needle.

Picking up a purl stitch

With the back of the work facing, put the hook through the dropped stitch from back to front. Place the hook around the thread immediately in front and draw through the dropped stitch. Continue until the same level is reached as the rest of the work and place the stitch on the left-hand needle.

UNPICKING MISTAKES

In the course of intricate pattern work, occasionally the number of stitches may vary from the original number. It is necessary to keep a careful check on the number of stitches so as not to throw out the whole pattern. When a mistake is discovered, careful unpicking is the best way to rectify the error. If this is done stitch by stitch no evidence of the unpicking will remain.

Unpicking knit stitches

Put left-hand needle through lower stitch. Pull right-hand needle out of the stitch above it and pull the yarn out with the right hand.

Unpicking purl stitches

With yarn at front on purl side, put left-hand needle in lower stitch, pull right-hand needle out of the stitch above and pull out yarn.

CASTING OFF

Follow the pattern as to which of three methods should be used for casting off. If no indication is given, cast off knitwise. Take care to have an even edge, because if it is too tight the edge will pucker. On most neck edges it is advisable to cast-off with the right-hand needle being one size larger than those used for working the body of the neckband. This will give it more elasticity.

Casting off knitwise

Knit the first two stitches. Put the end of left-hand needle into the front of the first stitch, lift it over second stitch and off the needle.

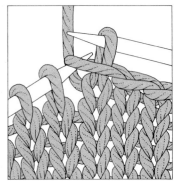

Knit another stitch and repeat process until one stitch remains. Break the yarn and draw it firmly through the last stitch.

Casting off purlwise and in rib

To cast off purlwise, purl the first two stitches, and lift the first stitch over the second and off the needle. Continue purling and casting off to the last stitch and fasten off the broken yarn. For a ribbed casting off, as used on most neck and arm bands, knit the first stitch, then purl the second. Lift the first stitch over the second and off the needle. Knit the third stitch and lift over the second. Continue in this manner until all the stitches are cast-off. Fasten off the last stitch with the end of the yarn.

Shaping

It is now time to learn how to shape a garment. Nearly every knitted garment includes some shaping, either for sleeves or necklines, or in the basic body shape. Shaping is done by either increasing or decreasing stitches or by a combination of both. Where the object is solely to shape a garment these techniques can be worked almost invisibly. However, they can also be used in a decorative way to create lacy and embossed stitch patterns.

DECREASING

This is the main method used to reduce the width of garments, especially for sleeve top and armhole shaping, and at the neckline. It is also the basis for many intricate, but decorative stitch patterns.

Knitting two stitches together

 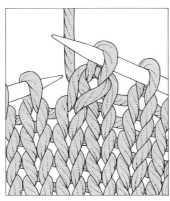

Put right-hand needle into front of second stitch and then front of first stitch, knitwise. Yarn around needle and pull through both stitches and drop both stitches off left-hand needle.

Purling two stitches together

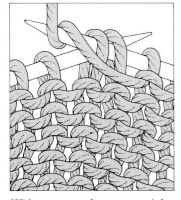 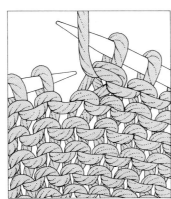

With yarn at front, put right-hand needle into the front of the first and then the second stitch, purlwise. Wind the yarn around the needle, and pull it through both the stitches, then drop them both off the left-hand needle at the same time.

Slipstitch decreasing, knitwise

With the yarn at the back of the work, slip the first stitch from the left- to the right-hand needle, knitwise. Do not knit it. Now knit the second stitch. With the left-hand needle, lift the first stitch over the second knitted stitch and off the needle.

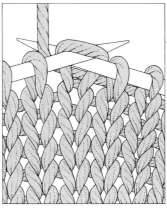 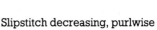

Slipstitch decreasing, purlwise

With the yarn at the front of the work, slip the first stitch from the left- to the right-hand needle, purlwise. Do not purl it. Purl the second stitch. Lift the first stitch over the second with the left-hand needle, and off the needle.

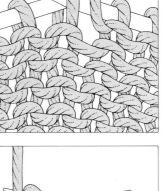 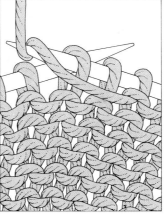 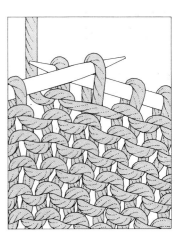

INCREASING STITCHES

The second most commonly used method of shaping knitted garments is by increasing the number of stitches, and it is also used extensively in intricate pattern designs, especially for lacy stitches. There are several methods of increasing stitches but the two most often used are the invisible and the decorative methods.

Invisible increasing

This is the simplest method of increasing. It is generally used to change the shape of a garment at the sides, but can be worked anywhere along a row just as successfully.

Two stitches from one knitwise

Knit into the front of the next stitch with the right-hand needle, but do not slip it off the left-hand needle. Now knit into the back of the same stitch with the right-hand needle, and slip the switch off the left-hand needle making two from one.

Two stitches from one purlwise

Purl into the front of next stitch but do not slip it off the left-hand needle. With right-hand needle purl into the front of this stitch again and then slip it off the left-hand needle.

Knitting into stitch below knitwise

With the right-hand needle knit into the loop immediately below the next stitch on the left-hand needle. Now knit into the next stitch on the left-hand needle in the normal way.

Knitting into stitch below purlwise

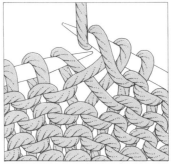 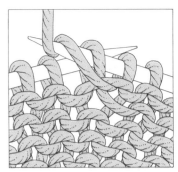

With right-hand needle purl into the loop immediately below the next stitch on left-hand needle. Now purl into the next stitch on the left-hand needle in the normal way.

Knitting into running thread below knitwise

With the left-hand needle pick up the loop which lies in front of it and keep it on the left-hand needle. Knit into the back of this loop and slip it off the left-hand needle. This method is sometimes called 'make one'.

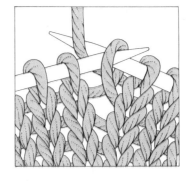 

Knitting into running thread below purlwise

With the left-hand needle pick up the loop which lies in front of it and keep it on the left-hand needle. Purl into the back of this loop and slip it off the left-hand needle.

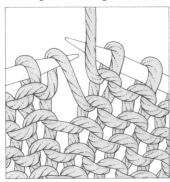

This beautifully worked baby's jacket illustrates how effectively the method of decorative increasing can be used. It has a particularly delicate effect as worked here in fine yarn and with thin needles. It may appear to be very intricate but the basic technique, as described here, is very easy to follow and well worth mastering.

Decorative increasing

In some patterns the increased stitch is featured as a decorative item, by creating a small hole with every increased stitch. The increased stitch is formed between two existing stitches by looping the yarn over the needle.

Yarn forward

To make a new stitch between two knit stitches, put the yarn in front. Put right-hand needle into next stitch knitwise. Pass yarn over right-hand needle, under the tip of the left-hand one, and around and under the tip of the right-hand needle again. Pull the loop through and slip stitch from left-hand needle. On the next row, in stocking stitch, purl into this new loop as usual.

Yarn round needle

To make a new stitch between two purl stitches, begin with the yarn at the front of the work, loop it around the right-hand needle and back to the front. Now purl the next stitch normally and pull off the left-hand needle. On the next row, in stocking stitch, knit into the new loop as usual. To make a stitch between a purl and a knit stitch, take the yarn from front over the needle to knit the next stitch, called 'yarn over needle'.

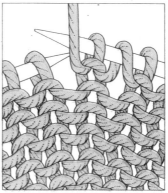

Advanced techniques

It is time to look at some techniques which require a little more skill but include the basic stitches that have already been learnt. Simple bobbles and cables are the basis for many complicated patterns, but they are not difficult to master. It is also necessary to learn colourwork techniques and how to make knitted buttonholes as these are often seen on cardigans and jackets and in baby clothing, and how to pick up stitches along the edges for forming collars, necklines and armbands.

CABLE

All forms of cable are worked on the principle of moving a number of stitches from one place to another in the same row. Up to two stitches at a time can be moved quite easily, using only two knitting needles, but when it is necessary to transfer more than this number, it is easier to use a short, double-pointed cable needle. The stitches to be moved are held on the cable needle, either at the front or the back of the work, until needed.

Simple cable knitwise

Take the right-hand needle around the back of the first stitch on the left-hand needle, and knit into the front of the second

stitch. Then knit into the front of the first stitch and slip both stitches off the left-hand needle together.

Simple cable purlwise

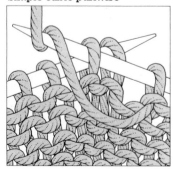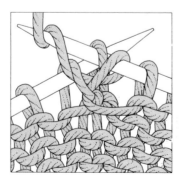

Take the right-hand needle in front of the first stitch on the left-hand needle and purl into the front of the second stitch.

Then purl into the front of the first stitch and slip both stitches off the left-hand needle at the same time.

Cabling with a cable needle

Cable twist to right: slip three stitches onto a cable needle and put at the front of the work. Knit the next three stitches and then knit the three stitches from the cable needle.

Cable twist to left: slip three stitches onto a cable needle and put at the back of the work. Knit the next three stitches and then knit the three stitches from the cable needle.

BOBBLES

The basis for making bobbles is always to make more than one stitch from the stitch where the bobble is desired, and then decrease back to the original stitch in the same or a later row.

To make a bobble

Knit to the position where the bobble is required. Make five stitches from the next stitch by knitting into the front then back of the stitch twice, and then knit into the front again. Turn and knit these five stitches, turn and purl the five stitches. With the left-hand needle lift second, third, fourth and fifth stitches over the first stitch and remove from the right-hand needle. Continue knitting until the position of the next bobble is reached and repeat the whole process.

BUTTONHOLES

Many patterns require buttonholes to be made. The two main methods are horizontal and vertical buttonholes used on the bands of jackets and cardigans. When small buttonholes are needed, such as on baby clothing, simple eyelet holes are ideal.

Eyelet buttonholes

Work to the position of the buttonhole. Bring the yarn forward between the needles to the front of the work and take it over the needle to knit the next two stitches together. On the next row, purl the yarn taken over. To make a channel for threading ribbon or cord, work a succession of eyelets across the row at the point where a channel is required.

Horizontal buttonholes

Knit to the position of the buttonhole and cast off the required number of stitches to fit the button size. Continue to the end of the row. On the next row, work to the stitch before the casting-off, knit into it twice and then cast-on one less number of stitches than were cast-off on the row before. Continue working until the position of the next buttonhole is reached, and then repeat the process.

Vertical buttonholes

Knit to the position of the buttonhole and then divide the work and knit each side separately. When each side is long enough to fit the button comfortably, continue to work across the whole row. Continue working until the position of the next buttonhole is reached and then repeat the whole process.

PICKING UP STITCHES

 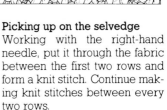

Picking up on the cast-off edge
Push the right-hand needle through the first edge stitch. Take the yarn under and over the needle and make a knit stitch. Continue making knit stitches in every stitch until right number exists.

Picking up on the selvedge
Working with the right-hand needle, put it through the fabric between the first two rows and form a knit stitch. Continue making knit stitches between every two rows.

COLOURWORK

Modern hand-knitting uses a great deal of colourwork, either to emphasize a pattern or in careful blending of colours, and in collage and graph knitting. Picture sweaters which incorporate several colours in the body of the work are especially popular. Although it may at first appear difficult to handle two or more balls of yarn at the same time, once stranding and weaving of colours has been mastered, the problem quickly disappears.

Slipstitch colourwork

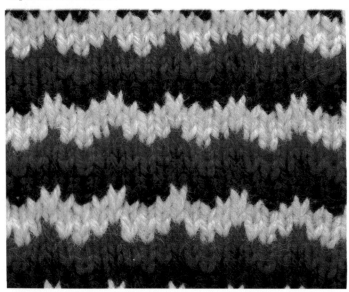

Slipstitch colourwork is a very easy way of creating interesting multicoloured patterns since it involves using only one colour in any row. The second colour is simply left at the side of the work until needed for a later row. The stitches not being worked in a row are slipped from the left-hand needle to the right-hand needle and the yarn in use is carried across the back of them. The pictures above show the front and back of a typical slipstitch pattern.

Joining in new colours

New colours can be joined in at the beginning of or during the row of knitting. It needs to be done smoothly and securely, so that no holes result where there is a join, especially in the middle of a knitted piece.

At the beginning of a row

Put the right-hand needle into the first stitch and with the first colour make a loop and then make one with the new colour over this needle. Finish the stitch by pulling these loops through in a normal way. To make more secure, work the next two stitches with both ends of the new yarn. At the end of the next row be careful to work the last three stitches as single stitches.

In the centre

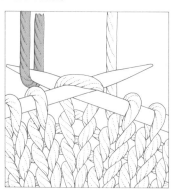

Knit to the position where the new colour is to be introduced. Put right-hand needle into the next stitch and with the new colour make a loop around the end of this needle. Make the stitch in the normal way, but work the next two stitches with both ends of the new yarn. When working the next row remember to work these as single stitches.

Stranding colours

After joining in the new colour in one of the above methods, work with the first colour and loosely carry the new yarn across the back of the work until it is needed. Change to the new colour and strand the first colour across the back until it is needed once more.

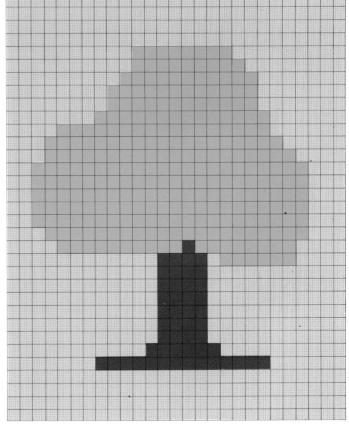

The tree has first been plotted onto a graph so that it can be easily knitted into the work. Each square represents one stitch. Read knit rows from right to left and purl rows from left to right.

Weaving colours knitwise

When the contrast yarn is carried across more than five stitches it must be woven into the back of the work. Keep first colour in the right hand and second in the left. Knit the first stitch in the usual way, but on the second and every alternate stitch put the right-hand needle into the stitch, loop the left-hand yarn across top of the needle, but work the stitch in the normal way with the first colour.

Weaving colours purlwise

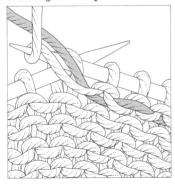 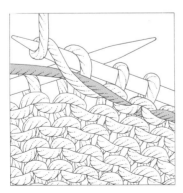

Insert the right-hand needle and make a loop with the right-hand yarn over the end of the needle. Pass the yarn to be woven over the top of the needle and purl normally. Alternatively, first place the yarn from the left hand in front of the needles and purl the stitch with the right-hand yarn.

Reading knitting patterns

Now that you have learnt the basic stitches and knitting techniques, it is time to think about making a garment. In deciding what to make you may either decide to buy a printed pattern or design something for yourself, but most people lack the confidence in their own ability and imagination to tackle the latter, at least at first.

SELECTING A PATTERN

When selecting a printed pattern careful consideration needs to be given to choosing a suitable design for your own level of ability so that it will be successful and encourage you to develop your knitting skills. If you are choosing your first pattern, try to select something which is not absolutely dependent on perfect sizing and shaping. As you learn to work with a smooth tension and feel at ease with pattern terminology you can then look to something more challenging. Also do not choose a very complicated cable or colourwork pattern for your first attempt – these too can be worked up to at a later date.

Check that the sizes stated include one which is suitable for your measurements. It will allow some room for movement when wearing the garment. If several sets of figures are given, the smallest one is always indicated first, and larger sizes will follow usually in brackets. It is a good idea to mark your own size wherever it is shown as you read through the pattern.

All printed patterns will specify all the requirements necessary to complete the garment. They will state the amount and type of yarn, needle sizes both for the bands and the body, the correct tension, body measurements, any notions, such as buttons or zippers, needed to complete the garment, and an explanation of any abbreviations used throughout the pattern.

CHOOSING THE YARN

Make sure the yarn you choose can be knitted up to the same tension as that of the pattern. Check the ball band or buy a sample ball and knit a tension square.

When buying yarn for a garment ensure that the whole quantity is from the one dye lot. Check the ball bands carefully as they will state both the colour number and dye lot number. Each dye lot differs in shade fractionally and there could be a marked line on the garment where the balls of different dye lots have been joined.

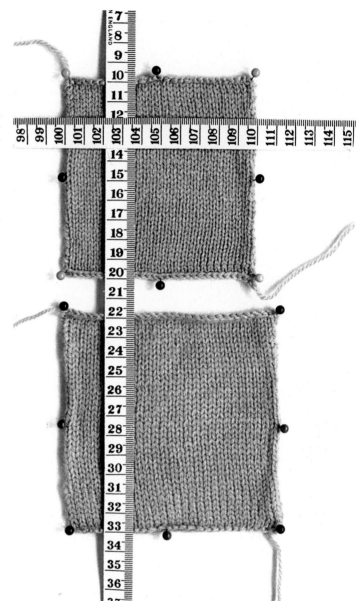

TENSION

The success of every knitted garment depends on using the correct tension, and you will never become a competent knitter until due consideration is given to this fact every time you commence a new piece of knitting. Tension does not simply mean even knitting, but indicates the number of stitches and rows over a given measurement, which is necessary to make the garment to the size as designed.

However experienced a knitter you are, it is essential to work a tension square in the stated yarn before commencing a pattern. Then at this stage you can assess if any adjustments need to be made in needle sizes or the design – before it is too late. The garment will only turn out to be the correct size if your tension is exactly the same as the one stated on the pattern.

Before starting a pattern, knit a tension square in the stated yarn and with the recommended needle size. Cast on a few more stitches than the figure given for the stitch tension and work a few more rows than the figure given for the row tension. Make sure that you knit in the stated stitch pattern as well.

When you have worked a square, lay it on a flat surface and mark out the suggested number of stitches and rows with pins. Do not start right at the edge stitch for these measurements. Now measure the distance between the pins. If you have too many stitches for the measurement, this means that your tension is too tight, and you should rework the square using a size larger needle. On the other hand if there are too few stitches, your tension is too loose, and a size smaller needle should be used to rework the tension square. It is necessary to continue experimenting with different needle sizes until the correct tension is achieved. You should also check the row tension at the same time, but it is easier to add a few rows to the depth of a garment, keeping the stitch pattern correct, than it is to adjust the width of a garment.

Another advantage of working a tension square is that it enables you to gain some experience with the stitch pattern used in your garment. It will speed up your work when you commence because you will be able to understand the terminology and abbreviations being used.

THE INSTRUCTIONS

After you have chosen the yarn and needles, and worked a tension square, it is time to commence the pattern. You will have already read the pattern with great care and marked the appropriate size you will be working. The pattern will indicate in which order the pieces are to be worked, and even though the choice may not be your own preference, it is advisable to stick to the order as printed. It is not uncommon to find instructions which relate to previously completed pieces for some necessary measurement. It is also advisable to join the pieces together in the order suggested because this may be relevant for some further work, such as neckbands or collars.

Try to make a habit of checking your work as you go along, especially if it is a complicated and repeated pattern. It is often easier for the eye to pick up a mistake during the course of a pattern than when the piece is completed. A careful check of the number of stitches is another indication that all is going according to plan. When you are checking the measurements of a piece of knitting do so on a flat surface and with a rigid measuring tape. Do not measure around curved edges, but place your tape measure at right angles to a straight edge of the rows.

Where graphs or stitch diagrams are used it must be remembered that they only show the right side of the work, and that each graph square represents one stitch. Therefore the odd numbered rows, or front side, should be worked from right to left, and the even numbered rows, or reverse side, should be worked from left to right. For left-handed knitters the patterns should be read in the reverse direction. When knitting on circular needles each round begins on the right-hand edge of each chart. Graphs are particularly popular with Fair Isle knitting and in collage or picture sweaters.

Another useful hint is to remember never to leave your knitting in the middle of a row, or if you have to leave the knitting for any length of time do not leave it in the middle of a piece. You will discover, when you recommence, an ugly ridge across the row where you stopped knitting, and it is virtually impossible to remove it.

When knitting in rows try, wherever possible, to join new balls in at the end of a row, as a knot in the middle of a row of knitting will only result in an unsightly hole. If it is unavoidable to have a mid-row join, and when knitting using circular needles, join the yarns by splicing the ends together as described on page 16.

ABBREVIATIONS

All knitting patterns use abbreviations to save space and time. They are usually explained in full detail at the beginning of each pattern. Abbreviations are generally the same in most printed patterns, but careful reading of their explanations can avoid any unnecessary mistakes.

The accompanying list of abbreviations needs to be studied carefully to enable you to use the following stitch patterns, and they are also used in the section of knitting projects. In some of the projects there are extra abbreviations that are relevant only to that particular pattern; in such cases these are explained at the beginning of the pattern.

alt	alternate	oz	ounces
approx	approximately	P	purl
beg	begin(ning)	psso	pass slipped stitch over
cm	centimetre(s)	p2sso	pass 2 slipped stitches over
dec	decreas(e)(ing)		
g	grammes	RH	right-hand
g st	garter stitch	RS	right side
in	inch(es)	sl	slip
inc	increas(e)(ing)	st(s)	stitch(es)
K	knit	st st	stocking stitch
LH	left-hand	tbl	through back of loop(s)
M1	make 1 by picking up loop between next st and st just worked and knitting into the back of it	tog	together
		yfwd	yarn forward
		yon	yarn over needle
		yrn	yarn round needle
mm	millimetres	WS	wrong side
no	number		

KEY TO STITCH SYMBOLS

These symbols are used in the stitch pattern charts on pages 26-37

* selvedge st (these can be ignored if no selvedge stitches are required)

O   K1

● P1

□ K1 tbl

■ P1 tbl

⋈ sl 1

⋈ sl 1 P-wise with yarn at back of work

⋈ sl 1 P-wise with yarn at front of work

+ yfwd or yrn or yon (to make 1 st)

⤸ work into front and back of st

↳ yrn, sl 1 P-wise

◇ K2 tog

◆ sl 1, K1, psso

⟩ P2 tog

⟨ P2 tog tbl

☆☆ P3 tog

⬈ sl 1, K2 tog, psso

⬉ sl 2, K2 tog, psso

∇ insert RH needle under 3 loose strands and K them tog with next st

⩔ (K1, yfwd, K1) all into next st

- cast off

⅄ make bobble: (K1, yfwd, K1, yfwd, K1) all into next st, turn, P5, turn, K5, sl 4th, 3rd, 2nd and 1st st over 5th st and off needle

⟋OO sl 1 st onto cable needle and hold at front, K2, then K1 from cable needle

OO⟍ sl 2 sts onto cable needle and hold at back, K1, then K2 from cable needle

O⟍OO sl 1 st onto cable needle and hold at back, K2, then K1 from cable needle

OO⟋OO sl 2 sts onto cable needle and hold at front, K2, then K2 from cable needle

OO⟍OO sl 2 sts onto cable needle and hold at back, K2, then K2 from cable needle

●⟍OO sl 1 st onto cable needle and hold at back, K2, then P1 from cable needle

OO⟋● sl 2 sts onto cable needle and hold at front, P1, then K2 from cable needle

OOOOO⟍OOOOO sl 5 sts onto cable needle and hold at back, K5, then K5 from cable needle

OOOOO⟋OOOOO sl 5 sts onto cable needle and hold at front, K5, then K5 from cable needle

OOO⟍OOO sl 3 sts onto cable needle and hold at back, K3, then K3 from cable needle

OOO⟋OOO sl 3 sts onto cable needle and hold at front, K3, then K3 from cable needle

Stitch patterns

The stitch patterns on the following pages are given in chart form. The key to the symbols used is on page 25. To follow the charts, read right-side rows (odd-numbered) from right to left and wrong-side rows (even-numbered) from left to right. The figures given in brackets represent the multiple of rows and stitches over which the pattern repeats. To work the patterns, cast on a multiple of the stitch figure, plus any extra stitches mentioned and, if required, selvedge stitches.

One by one rib (2 rows and 2 sts, plus 1 extra)

Ridge stitch (8 rows and any number of sts)

Irish moss stitch (4 rows and 2 sts, plus 1 extra)

Sailor's rib (4 rows and 5 sts, plus 1 extra)

Berry stitch (8 rows and 4 sts)

Moss stitch (2 rows and 2 sts, plus 1 extra)

Basketweave (8 rows and 8 sts, plus 5 extra)

Aran patterns

Traditionally, Aran patterns are produced by beautiful combinations of cables, bobbles and honeycomb stitches. They are worked in the thick, natural, unbleached Aran wool, which makes ideal sweaters, jackets, scarves and hats.

Grapes (12 rows and 20 sts, plus 1 extra)

Embossed diamond (20 rows and 18 sts)

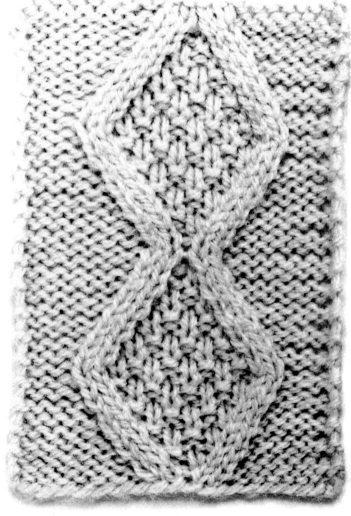

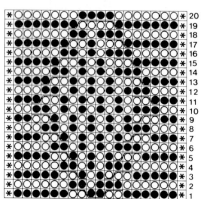

Honeycomb cable (8 rows and 8 sts)

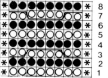

Basket cable (12 rows and 30 sts)

Horseshoe pattern (12 rows and 16 sts)

Braided cable (6 rows and 15 sts, plus 1 extra)

Plait cable (8 rows and 19 sts)

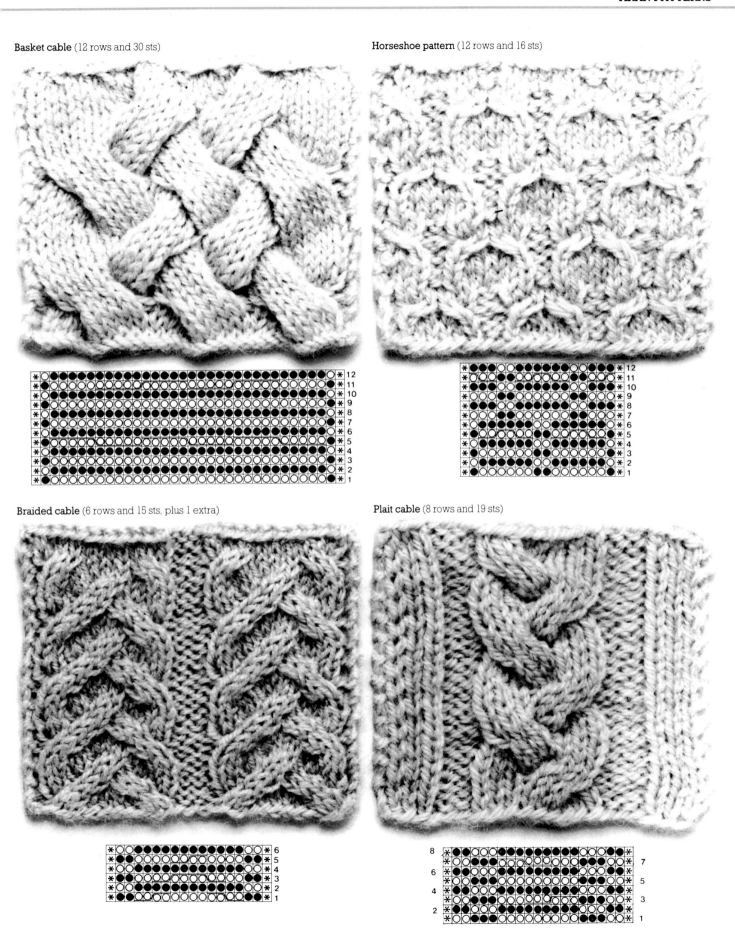

Simple colourwork

Most of these designs form the basis of Norwegian, Fair Isle and Shetland knitting, where patterns are worked in stocking stitch in two or more colours. The graphs below each pattern clearly show how to make each one. Each square represents one stitch.

Lily pattern (6 rows and 8 sts)

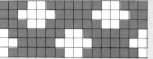

Diamond stitch (25 rows and 10 sts)

Windowpane (18 rows and 12 sts)

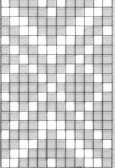

Check pattern (8 rows and 8 sts)

Diagonals (10 rows and 5 sts)

Fair Isle border (18 rows and 4 sts)

Chevron pattern (16 rows and 10 sts)

Lacy patterns

These illustrate some of the great variety of lacy patterns available. They have a soft and delicate effect when knitted in fine yarn and using thin needles, but this effect would be lost in thick yarn and needles. The basic stitch technique is decorative increasing.

Plait pattern (4 rows and 12 sts)

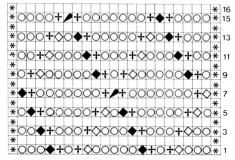

Candle pattern (16 rows and 10 sts; P every WS row)

Diamond eyelet (16 rows and 10 sts; P every WS row)

Fancy trellis (8 rows and 7 sts)

Leaf pattern (12 rows and 18 sts)

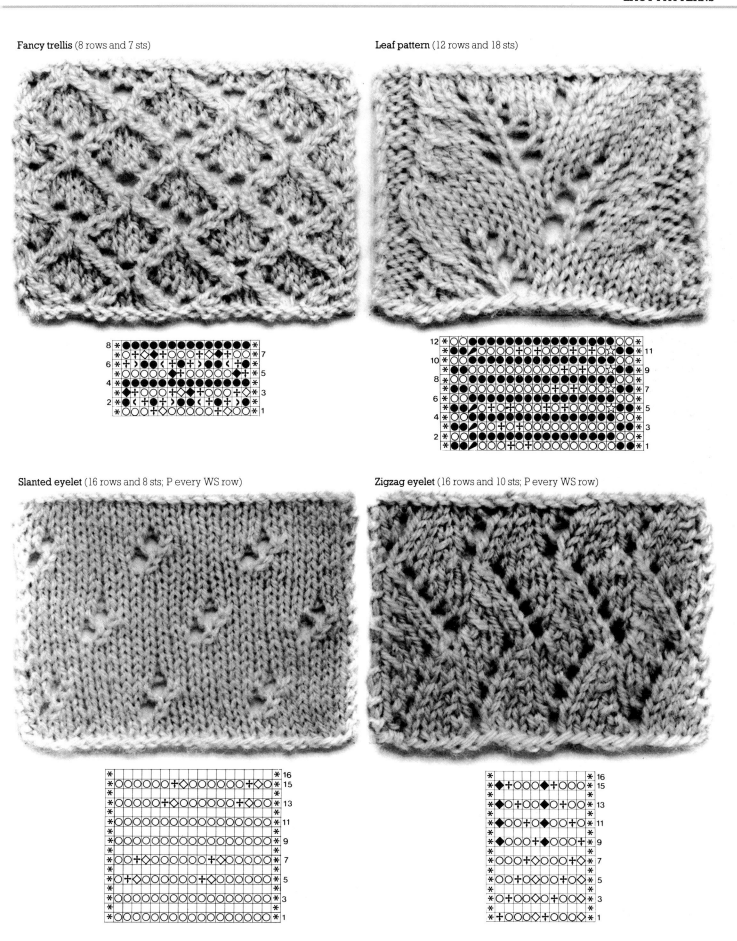

Slanted eyelet (16 rows and 8 sts; P every WS row)

Zigzag eyelet (16 rows and 10 sts; P every WS row)

Slipstitch colourwork

These patterns are a more complicated form of the colourwork which uses the technique of slipping stitches in regular patterns. The graph under each one has each row numbered and the accompanying letters (A, B and C) indicate where the different colours are to be introduced. Attention is needed to start these patterns correctly but they are not very difficult once established.

Slipstitch rib (4 rows and 6 sts)

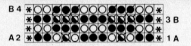

Interlacing stripes (18 rows and 8 sts, plus 3 extra)

Chequer stitch (14 rows and 6 sts, plus 3 extra)

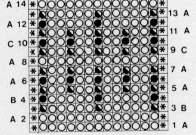

Florentine stitch (12 rows and 24 sts, plus 2 extra)

Diamond slipstitch (12 rows and 6 sts, plus 5 extra)

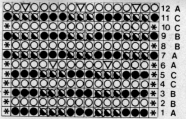

Greek tile pattern (20 rows and 10 sts, plus 2 extra)

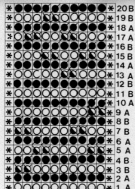

Ricrac pattern (16 rows and 6 sts)

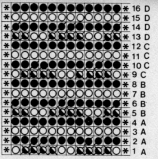

Lacy edgings

Unfortunately these delightful and decorative edgings are not seen as often as could be. They utilize decorative increasing and decreasing techniques and could be used effectively on hems, collars and cuffs, and as attractive finishings on many soft furnishings around the home. To appreciate these light and airy designs they should be worked in fine yarn.

Seashore edging (14 rows and 16 sts)

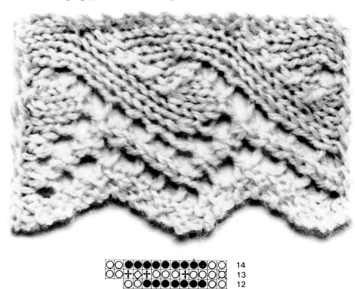

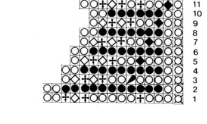

Eyelet border (22 rows and 16 sts, plus 3 extra)

Faggot and scallop edging (20 rows and 13 sts)

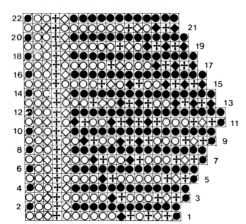

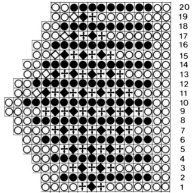

Fir tree edging (6 rows and 21 sts)

Saw-toothed edging (14 rows and 17 sts)

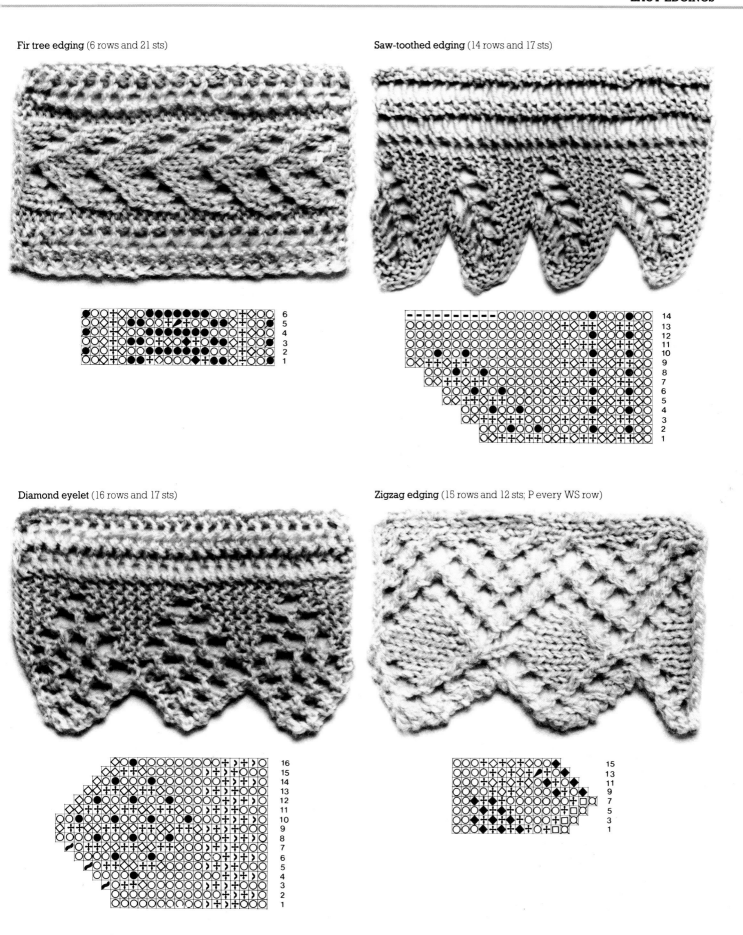

Diamond eyelet (16 rows and 17 sts)

Zigzag edging (15 rows and 12 sts; P every WS row)

Finishing off

The finishing and sewing together of a knitted garment is often thought to be tedious, but a little care taken at this stage will make the difference to the whole success of the finished garment. The loose ends of the wool, at either side of the knitting, should be darned into the back of the work with a wool needle. Then the yarn may be trimmed close to the fabric.

Before deciding whether to press the work, it is necessary to read the ball bands carefully to see if the yarn is suitable for pressing. Here you will also find advice as to the correct temperature for pressing. Pressing is not recommended on textured work, mohair, acrylic or glitter yarns, or any ribbed bands, which would loose their elasticity if pressed.

Turn the piece right side down on a padded surface. Pin the edges to the correct shape, also checking the measurements. Cover the knitting with a damp cloth for cotton and wool, and a dry one for nylon. Lower the iron, but do not pull it across the fabric. Lift the iron and lower it gently onto another section of the work. Leave the piece until the yarn is completely dry.

SEWING UP

Follow the pattern carefully as to the order in which the pieces should be sewn together, as this may be relevant to any further work, such as neckbands or collars. The two main methods of joining the edges are with an invisible seam or a back stitch seam. The latter is the stronger seam and is best when working against the grain of the fabric. When sleeves are sewn in, the stitches should not be so tight that there is no room for stretching.

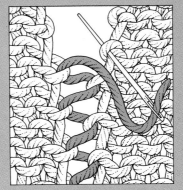 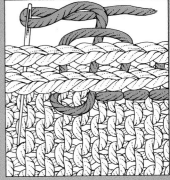

Invisible seam
With right sides of the fabric together, match the edges. Secure the yarn at the bottom of the seam. The needle must be passed under the thread between the first two edge stitches. Now pick up the next thread on the opposite side and firmly draw the two edges together, without any puckering. Continue along the seam.

Back stitch seam
With right sides facing, match the edges. Secure the yarn at the bottom. Work from right to left over one knitted stitch at a time. Take yarn across one stitch at the back and through to front. Take yarn back to the right by one stitch through to the back, to the left by two stitches and to the front. Continue till the seam is complete.

LAUNDRY SYMBOLS

Careful reading of the ball bands is invaluable when it comes to the aftercare of a knitted garment. They show information, using international symbols, as illustrated below, for washing, ironing, bleaching and dry cleaning.

The wash tub indicates suitability for washing and the correct water temperatures. The upper figure indicates the automatic washing cycle which is suitable for machine washable yarns. The lower figure indicates the water temperature for hand washing. If the yarn is only suitable for hand washing a hand will be shown in the tub, and if the tub is crossed through the yarn is then only suitable for dry cleaning.

When bleach can be used a triangle with the letters CL inside will appear, but generally the triangle will be crossed out as most yarns cannot be bleached.

Suitable ironing temperatures are shown by an iron containing three dots for hot, two dots for warm, and one dot for a cool iron. An iron crossed out indicates that pressing is not recommended. Extreme care should be given to a garment knitted with a mixture of yarns, and the lowest temperature shown on the ball bands should be used.

For dry cleaning a circle appears with the letters A, P and F, which refer to the different dry cleaning solvents. A crossed out circle indicates that the garment cannot be dry cleaned.

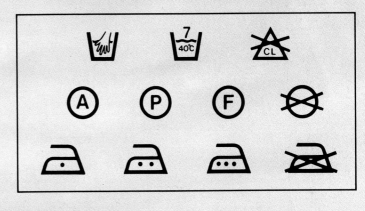

Creative knitting

Placing beads

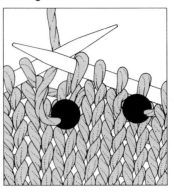 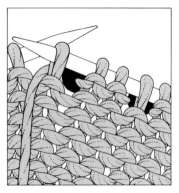

With a little imagination and patience any competent knitter can create completely original garments. Most people are only lacking in confidence in their own ability and this inhibits their creative ability. But today with such a variety of yarns and other knitting materials available to the hand-knitter more encouragement should be given to those trying to be inventive.

Initially it is not necessary to aim at designing your own knitwear but to work up to this achievement gradually. One step in this direction is to alter fairly basic knitwear patterns by the addition of new trimmings and finishings such as embroidery, appliqué or any number of hand-made trimmings.

Embroidery can easily be worked onto knitted fabrics to enhance the shape and texture. Stitches should be applied loosely to allow for the stretch in the garment, and can directly follow the knitted stitches or be applied in a completely free manner. It is better to start working from a chart using the technique of counted thread embroidery. But remember that as each knitted stitch is not exactly square, as graph paper, the finished effect will be slightly flatter. The simplest embroidery stitches are usually the most effective such as running, chain, satin, blanket, stem, feather, cross stitch and french knots.

Other needlework techniques such as quilting, appliqué and smocking can be used just as successfully. Swiss darning is also a popular method of applying motifs, and they appear as if knitted along with the rest of the garment. It is best to do this with yarn or thread of a similar thickness, in order to cover each stitch completely.

Swiss darning

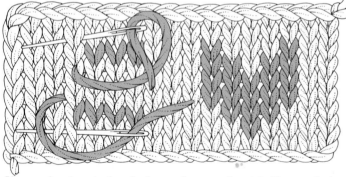

Always begin at the bottom right-hand corner of the motif. Secure the thread at the back of the work and bring the needle through to the front at the centre of the base of the first stitch to be covered. Take the needle behind the base of the stitch above from right to left and pull the yarn through. Now push the needle back through the centre of the base of the original stitch and bring it out through the centre of the base of the next stitch to be covered. Carry on in this way until the motif is completed, using one or more colours as required.

Many decorative trimmings can be made to add interest to a fairly plain garment, such as pompons, tassels, bobbles, strips of French knitting and ridges. For example, oddments of yarn can be made into narrow tubes of French knitting and then hand-sewn onto a garment. This is usually worked on a knitting Nancy or using something like a wooden cotton reel with four small nails inserted around the central hole.

This is one of the easiest ways of working beads into a knitted fabric and is suitable even for very small beads, placing them so that they will not slip through to the back of the work. The beads can be placed when working either wrong-side or right-side rows. Work to the bead position then take the yarn forward or back between the needles to the right side of the work. Slip the next stitch then push the bead down the yarn close to the work. Take the yarn back or forward to the wrong side and work as usual to the next bead position.

Other small trimmings can be successfully attached to a garment, as long as they can be held securely in place. They look most effective when placed on a smooth background of stocking stitch, but beading can be worked in to complement the knitted pattern. Beads can either be sewn onto or knitted into a garment, but it is necessary to work out their order of placement beforehand, ideally on graph paper. They should be evenly placed along the length of the row, with several plain rows between each row of decoration, so that the objects will lie flat against the surface. Thread the beads onto the yarn before beginning to knit and work them into the knitting as you go along, as shown above.

Another exciting dimension of modern hand-knitting which offers a great deal of scope for adaptation and creative work is in collage or colourwork. But it can be confusing to try to work with several different balls of wool at once and the resulting tangle at the back of the work can quite easily be avoided by using small wool bobbins. These can either be bought in a yarn supply shop or made yourself, cut out from stiff cardboard. Wind the yarn around the centre of each bobbin and through the slit at the top, which will prevent it unravelling. Do this before you start to knit and then they will simply hang from the back of the work without tangling, and avoid the need to strand the different yarns across the back of the fabric.

Designing your own garments can be both enjoyable and rewarding, allowing you to create something original for your pleasure. It requires a little work and attention to detail to be successful.

Firstly decide on the basic shape, colour, yarn and stitch to be used for your design. Buy a ball of the yarn and knit a tension square. This will enable you to work out the number of stitches and rows to fit your pattern. Then make a free-hand sketch of the design, followed by a scale drawing on squared paper. On this, each square will represent one stitch, but again remember that knitted stitches are not exactly square. Take care to check that the total number of stitches in each row is a multiple of your basic stitch pattern. An additional 5 cm (2 in) added to your basic measurements should be sufficient to allow for movement.

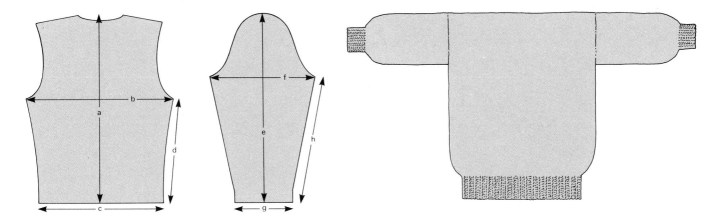

The sketches above with their accompanying measurements show what is needed to work out an accurate design.

(a) back length
(b) bust measurement
(c) lower edge measurement
(d) underarm length
(e) outer sleeve length
(f) width at upper arm
(g) cuff measurement
(h) sleeve seam

The other thing to consider when working out your design on graph paper is the shaping. This is important to ensure a well-fitting garment. The basic shaping on the body begins at the armhole. For a set-in sleeve the shaping is over the first 8 cm (3 in) with an acute start, and more gradual tapering into a gentle curve. On the body for raglan sleeves, the same initial acute decreasing is used but thereafter the stitches are decreased at a regular rate until only the number of stitches to be included in the neckline remain.

Shoulder shaping is also important on the body of the garment. It begins about 2.5 cm (1 in) below the finished length, and on each side is usually done in three equal steps.

Sleeves need regular increasing in their shape along the entire length to the underarm. The increasing should be done at each end of the same row at regular intervals up to the armhole. The shaping for the top of a set-in sleeve should decrease acutely to start with, giving way to a gradual curve to match the shaping on the underarm section on the body of the garment. The final number of stitches on the top of the set-in sleeve to be cast-off, should not be longer than 7.5 cm (3 in) or it will pucker along the shoulder line when sewn in. For raglan sleeves the decreasing must initially match that on the body of the garment, then be at regular intervals so that it fits neatly with the matching edge on the body without stretching.

For a basic round neckline, the shaping should commence 5 cm (2 in) below the back neckline, each shoulder being worked separately. The number of stitches for the shoulder shaping should be the same as those on the back. The remaining stitches on the centre front should be used for gradual shaping at the neck edge. A V-neckline usually starts at the same time as the armhole shaping, but may be shortened if so desired. Each shoulder should be worked separately, with gradual but regular decreasing until the same number of stitches remain for the shoulder shaping as were used for the shaping on the back of the garment.

If a traditionally tailored garment is not desired, a great deal of this shaping is unnecessarily cumbersome for first designs. Using softer yarns and more attention to texture, it is easy to design modern knitwear based on a number of rectangles joined together.

Using a basic sweater shape of four rectangles, adaptations can be made for a waistcoat, a dress, coat or cardigan. The easiest skirt design is made from a single rectangle with elastic threaded through a hem at the waist and a plain or fancy hem at the bottom.

For a sweater, base your design on four straight rectangles, two for the body and two for the sleeves. No shaping is necessary on any of the four pieces. Innumerable varieties can be imagined by changing the stitch pattern or colour or yarn, different necklines and hems, the addition of pockets, collars or yokes. A textured garment can be created by using a collection of different yarns, as long as the tension square has been knitted to check the measurements for the desired shape. For a cardigan or front opening coat the neck edge on both fronts must be shaped at the top.

AFTER-CARE

Considering the amount of time and skill taken in making a knitted garment, it is worth paying attention to after-care in order to keep it looking its best. Incorrect washing and pressing can ruin a beautiful hand-knitted garment. Careful reading of the ball bands will give the basic information such as water and ironing temperatures, and suitability for hand-washing or dry cleaning. (See page 39 for international laundry symbols and their meaning.)

Washing Always use warm, never hot, water and a washing detergent specially manufactured for cleaning knitwear. Do not soak hand-knitted garments, and avoid the need for this with frequent and brief washes. When wet, never lift the garment by the shoulders, as it is very easy for the weight to distort the shape. In the final rinse water, add fabric conditioner, so that the natural pile of the yarn is released. After all the soap has been carefully removed by repeated rinsing, gently squeeze out the excess water.

Drying This should be done on a flat surface, away from direct heat and sunlight. Ideally, place the wet garment on a newspaper which has been covered by a thick, clean towel. Pat out any creases and leave until dry. A final airing will be necessary, preferably on an outdoor clothes line. To prevent peg marks on a garment, thread a clean pair of nylon tights through the two sleeves and neck, and peg the tights onto the line.

Pressing If the washing and drying have been carried out carefully, pressing should not be necessary. If it is still thought desirable check the ball band for the correct temperature setting for the iron, and follow the same instructions for pressing as given for the making-up of a garment, remembering never to press the seams or the bands.

Wear and tear The two most common signs of wear and tear are small balls of fibre forming on the surface of a garment and snagging. The small balls can be removed with a specially designed comb which can be bought from a haberdashery department. To remove snags use a blunt-ended needle and pull the snag through to the reverse side. Gently adjust the stitch to its original shape and size and knot the end at the back.

ARAN SWEATERS
LACY MOHAIR SWEATER

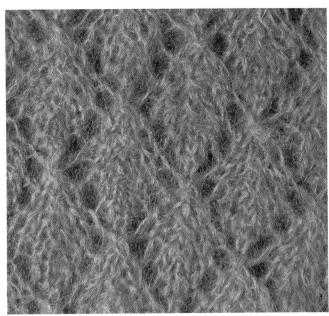

Lacy Mohair Sweater (page 43)

MEASUREMENTS
To fit bust: 91-96 cm (36-38 in)
Length from shoulder: 70 cm (27½ in)
Sleeve seam: 44 cm (17½ in)
Instructions are given for the smaller size first with the larger size in the following square brackets.

MATERIALS
350 g (14 oz) mohair
1 pair each of 3¾ mm (no 4), 5 mm (no 7) and 6 mm (no 9) knitting needles

TENSION
15 sts and 18 rows to 10 cm (4 in) over lace pattern on 6 mm (no 9) needles

BACK
With 3¾ mm (no 4) needles, cast on 74 sts. Work in K1, P1 rib for 15 cm (6 in), inc 1 st at end of last row. (75 sts)
Change to 5 mm (no 7) needles and P 1 row.
Change to 6 mm (no 9) needles and work in lace pattern as follows:
1st row. (RS) Sl 1, K2 tog, K2, *yrn, K1, yrn, K2, sl 1, K2 tog, psso, K2; repeat from * to last 6 sts, yrn, K1, yrn, K2, sl 1, K1, psso, K1.
2nd and every alt row. P.
3rd row. Sl 1, K2 tog, K1, *yrn, K3, yrn, K1, sl 1, K2 tog, psso, K1; repeat from * to last 7 sts, yrn, K3, yrn, K1, sl 1, K1, psso, K1.
5th row. Sl 1, K2 tog, *yrn, K5, yrn, sl 1, K2 tog, psso; repeat from * to last 8 sts, yrn, K5, yrn, sl 1, K1, psso, K1.
7th row. Sl 1, K1, *yrn, K2, sl 1, K2 tog, psso, K2, yrn, K1; repeat from * to last st, K1.
9th row. Sl 1, K2, *yrn, K1, sl 1, K2 tog, psso, K1, yrn, K3; repeat from * to end.
11th row. Sl 1, K3, *yrn, sl 1, K2 tog, psso, yrn, K5, repeat from * ending last repeat K4 instead of K5.
12th row. P.
These 12 rows form the pattern repeat. Continue in pattern until work measures 49.5 cm (19½ in).
Shape armholes
Keeping pattern correct, cast off 3 sts at beg of next 2 rows, then 2 sts at beg of following 6 rows. (57 sts)**

Work straight until work measures 68 cm (27 in), ending with a WS row.
Shape neck and shoulder
Next row. Pattern 26 sts, turn, leaving remaining sts on spare needle.
Cast off 4 sts at beg of next 3 rows, then 5 sts at beg of following row. Cast off 4 sts at beg of next row. Cast off remaining 5 sts.
Rejoin yarn to sts on spare needle at inner edge. Cast off 5 sts, pattern to end. Now complete to match first side of neck reversing shapings.

FRONT
Work as given for back to **.
Continue straight until work measures 65.5 cm (26 in) ending with a WS row.
Shape neck and shoulder
Next row. Pattern 27 sts, turn, leaving remaining sts on spare needle.
Next row. Cast off 3 sts, pattern to end.
Next row. Pattern to end.
Repeat the last 2 rows twice more. Now cast off 2 sts at beg of next row and 4 sts at beg of following row. Cast off 2 sts at beg of next row, then 5 sts at beg of following row.
Next row. Pattern to end.
Cast off remaining 5 sts.
Rejoin yarn to inner edge of sts on spare needle. Cast off 3 sts, pattern to end. Now complete to match first side of neck reversing shapings.

SLEEVES
With 3¾ mm (no 4) needles, cast on 42 sts. Work in K1, P1 rib for 10 cm (4 in).
Next row. Rib 4, (inc 1 into next st, rib 1) to last 4 sts, rib 4. (59 sts)
Change to 5 mm (no 7) needles and P 1 row.
Change to 6 mm (no 9) needles and continue in lace pattern as given for back until work measures 44 cm (17½ in).
Shape top
Cast off 3 sts at beg of next 2 rows, then 2 sts at beg of following 6 rows. Dec 1 st at beg of next 14 rows. Now cast off 2 sts at beg of next 2 rows, then 5 sts at beg of following 2 rows.
Cast off remaining 13 sts.

NECKBAND
With 3¾ mm (no 4) needles, cast on 176 sts. Work 10 rows in K1, P1 rib.
Next row. Cast off 48 sts, rib 90 sts including st used in casting off, cast off 38 sts.
Cast off remaining 90 sts.

MAKING UP
Do not press.
Join side, shoulder and sleeve seams. Set in sleeves.
With RS of work facing, sew cast-off 90 sts of neckband to neck edge, leaving 6.5 cm (2¾ in) free at front. Knot ties.

Aran Sweaters (page 42)

MEASUREMENTS
Child's sweater
To fit chest: 61-66 cm (24-26 in)
Width all round: 70 cm (27½ in)
Sleeve seam: 33 cm (13 in)

Man's sweater
To fit chest: 97-102 cm (38-40 in)
Width all round: 108 cm (42½ in)
Sleeve seam: 47 cm (20 in)
Instructions are given for the child's size first with those for the man's size in the following square brackets.

MATERIALS
500 g (20 oz) [1250 g (50 oz)] Aran-weight wool
1 pair 4½ mm (no 6) knitting needles
1 cable needle

TENSION
Each square measures 11.5 cm (4½ in) [18 cm (7 in)]

EXTRA ABBREVIATIONS
C4B – cable 4 back: sl next 2 sts onto cable needle and hold at back of work, K2, then K2 from cable needle.
C4F – cable 4 front: sl next 2 sts onto cable needle and hold at front of work, K2, then K2 from cable needle.

SQUARE 1 (make 14)
Cast on 24 [34] sts. K4 [6] rows, inc 4 sts evenly across last row. (28 [38] sts). Now continue in honeycomb pattern as follows:
1st row. (RS) K.
2nd and every alt row. K2 [3], P to last 2 [3] sts, K2 [3].
3rd row. K2 [3], *C4B, C4F; repeat from * to last 2 [3] sts, K2 [3].
5th row. As 1st row.
7th row. K2 [3], *C4F, C4B; repeat from * to last 2 [3] sts, K2 [3].
8th row. As 2nd row.
Repeat these 8 rows 2 [3] times more, then the first 1 [5] rows again.
Next row. K to end, dec 4 sts evenly across the row. K 3 [5] rows. Cast off.

SQUARE 2 (make 14)
Cast on 24 [34] sts. K4 [6] rows, inc 1 st in centre of last row (25 [35] sts). Now continue in fish net pattern as follows:
1st row. (RS) K6 [7], (P1, K7) 2 [3] times, P1, K2 [3].
2nd row. K2 [3], P1, K1, (P5, K1, P1, K1) 2 [3] times, P3, K2 [3].
3rd row. K4 [5], (P1, K3) to last 5 [6] sts, P1, K4 [5].
4th row. K2 [3], P3, (K1, P1, K1, P5) 2 [3] times, K1, P1, K2 [3].
5th row. K2 [3], (P1, K7) 2 [3] times, P1, K6 [7].
6th row. As 4th row.
7th row. As 3rd row.
8th row. As 2nd row.
Repeat these 8 rows 2 [3] times more, then the first 1 [5] rows again. K 4 [6] rows, dec 1 st in centre of 1st row.
Cast off.

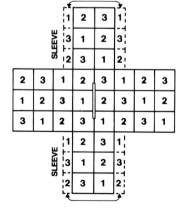

Assembly diagram for Aran squares: (1) honeycomb pattern, (2) fish net pattern, (3) trinity stitch.

SQUARE 3 (make 14)

Cast on 24 [34] sts. K4 [6] rows. Continue in trinity stitch as follows:

1st row. (RS) K2 [3], P to last 2 [3] sts, K2 [3].

2nd row. K2 [3], *(K1, P1, K1) all into next st, P3 tog; repeat from * to last 2 [3] sts, K2 [3].

3rd row. As 1st row.

4th row. K2 [3], *P3 tog, (K1, P1, K1) all into next st; repeat from * to last 2 [3] sts, K2 [3].

Repeat these 4 rows 4 [8] times more, then the first 2 [0] rows again. K 5 [7] rows. Cast off.

MAKING UP

Do not press. Using a flat seam join squares as shown in diagram, first joining back and front squares.

Now join 9 squares of each sleeve, fold then join sleeve seam. Set in sleeves.

Join side seams.

Cotton Sweaters (page 47)

MEASUREMENTS

To fit chest: 81 cm (32 in) [86 cm (34 in):91 cm (36 in):96 cm (38 in): 102 cm (40 in):107 cm (42 in)]
Length from shoulder: 63 cm (25 in) [63 cm (25 in): 66 cm (26 in): 66 cm (26 in):69 cm (27¼ in)]
Sleeve seam: 48cm (19in) [48cm (19 in):50 cm (19½ in):50 cm (19½ in):52 cm (20½ in):52 cm (20½ in)]
Instructions are given for the smallest size first with larger sizes in the following square brackets.

MATERIALS

550 g (22 oz) [550 g (22 oz):600 g (24 oz):650 g (26 oz):700 g (28 oz): 750 g (30 oz)] medium-weight cotton yarn
1 pair each 2¾ mm (no 2) and 3¼ mm (no 3) knitting needles
Set of four 2¾ mm (no 2) needles pointed at both ends
1 cable needle

TENSION

24 sts and 32 rows to 10 cm (4 in) over st st on 3¼ mm (no 3) needles

EXTRA ABBREVIATIONS

cr5 – cross 5: sl next 2 sts onto cable needle and hold at front of work, K2, P1, then K2 from cable needle

cr3R – cross 3 right: sl next st onto cable needle and hold at back of work, K2, then P1 from cable needle

cr3L – cross 3 left: sl next 2 sts onto cable needle and hold at front of work, P1, then K2 from cable needle

C6B – cable 6 back: sl next 3 sts onto cable needle and hold at back of work, K3, then K3 from cable needle

C6F – cable 6 front: sl next 3 sts onto cable needle and hold at front of work, K3, then K3 from cable needle

BACK

With 2¾ mm (no 2) needles, cast on 103 [107:113:117:123:127] sts.

1st row. K1, *P1, K1; repeat from * to end.

2nd row. P1, *K1, P1; repeat from * to end.

Repeat these 2 rows for 5 cm (2 in), ending with a 1st row.

Next row. Rib 3 [1:3:1:3:1], *inc 1 into next st, rib 4; repeat from * to last 5 [1:5:1:5:1] sts, inc 1 into next st, rib 4 [0:4:0:4:0]. (123 [129:135:141:147:153] sts.)

Change to 3¼ mm (no 3) needles and continue in pattern as follows:

1st row. K9 [11:13:15:17:19], *P2, K6, P6, cr5, P6, K6, P2*, K39 [41:43:45:47:49], repeat from * to * again, K to end.

2nd row. P9 [11:13:15:17:19], *K2, P6, K6, P2, K1, P2, K6, P6, K2*, P39 [41:43:45:47:49], repeat from * to * again, P to end.

3rd row. K9 [11:13:15:17:19], *P2, C6B, P5, cr3R, K1, cr3L, P5, C6F, P2*, K39 [41:43:45:47:49], repeat from * to * again, K to end.

4th row. K9 [11:13:15:17:19], *K2, P6, K5, P2, K1, P1, K1, P2, K5, P6, K2*, K39 [41:43:45:47:49], repeat from * to * again, K to end.

5th row. P9 [11:13:15:17:19], *P2, K6, P4, cr3R, K1, P1, K1, cr3L, P4, K6, P2*, P39 [41:43:45:47:49], repeat from * to * again, P to end.

6th row. K9 [11:13:15:17:19], *K2, P6, K4, P2, K1, (P1, K1) twice, P2, K4, P6, K2*, K39 [41:43:45:47:49], repeat from * to * again, K to end.

These 6 rows form the ridge pattern at edges and centre and establish the cable panels. Keeping ridge pattern correct, continue with cable panels as follows:

7th row. *P2, K6, P3, cr3R, K1, (P1, K1) twice, cr3L, P3, K6, P2*.

8th row. *K2, P6, K3, P2, K1, (P1, K1) 3 times, P2, K3, P6, K2*.

9th row. *P2, C6B, P2, cr3R, K1, (P1, K1) 3 times, cr3L, P2, C6F, P2*.

10th row. *K2, P6, K2, P2, K1, (P1, K1) 4 times, P2, K2, P6, K2*.

11th row. *P2, K6, P2, cr3L, P1, (K1, P1) 3 times, cr3R, P2, K6, P2*.

12th row. As 8th row.

13th row. *P2, K6, P3, cr3L, P1, (K1, P1) twice, cr3R, P3, K6, P2*.

14th row. As 6th row.

15th row. *P2, C6B, P4, cr3L, P1, K1, P1, cr3R, P4, C6F, P2*.

16th row. As 4th row.

17th row. *P2, K6, P5, cr3L, P1, cr3R, P5, K6, P2*.

18th row. As 2nd row.

These 18 rows form the pattern repeat for the cable panels. Keeping panels and ridge pattern correct continue until work measures 43 cm (17 in) [43 cm (17 in):44 cm (17½ in): 44 cm (17½ in):45 cm (17¾ in):45 cm (17¾ in)], ending with a WS row.

Shape armholes

Cast off 4 sts at beg of next 2 rows. (115 [121:127:133:139:145] sts.)

Work straight until the work measures 63 cm (25 in) [63 cm (25in):66 cm (26 in):66 cm (26 in): 269 cm (27¼ in):69 cm (27¼ in)], ending with a WS row.

Shape shoulders

Cast off 39 [42:44:47:49:52] sts loosely at beg of next 2 rows. Leave remaining 37 [37:39:39: 41:41] sts on a spare needle.

FRONT

Work as given for the back until the front measures 40 cm (15¾ in) [40 cm (15¾ in):41 cm (16 in):41 cm (16 in):42 cm (16½ in):42 cm (16½ in)], ending with a WS row.

Shape neck

Next row. Pattern 61 [64:67:70: 73:76]sts, turn, leaving remaining sts on a spare needle, pattern to end.

Next row. Pattern to last 3 sts, K2 tog, K1.

Pattern 7 rows, dec 1 st at neck edge as before on 4th row.

Shape armhole

Next row. Cast off 4 sts, pattern to last 3 sts, K2 tog, K1.

Keeping armhole edge straight, continue to dec at neck edge as before on every following 4th row until 39 [42:44:47:49:52] sts remain. Work straight until front matches back to shoulder, ending with a WS row. (Continued on page 48.)

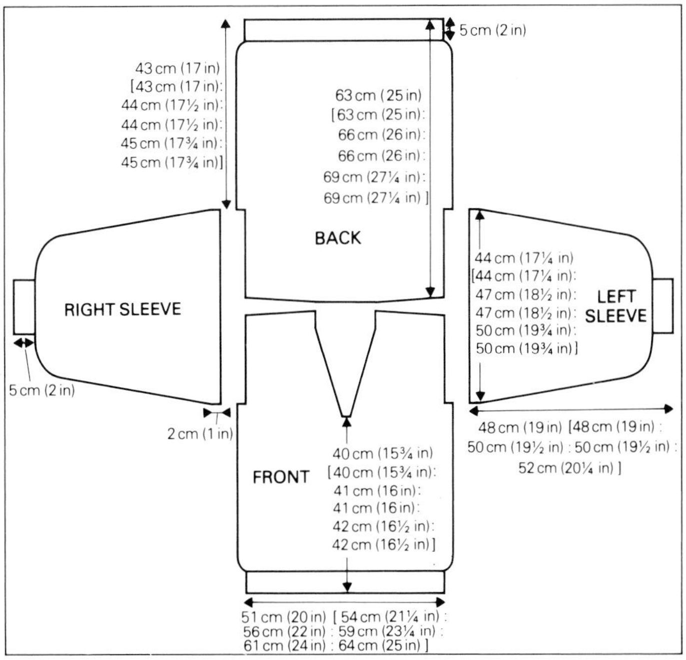

43 cm (17 in) [43 cm (17 in): 44 cm (17½ in): 44 cm (17½ in): 45 cm (17¾ in): 45 cm (17¾ in)]

5 cm (2 in)

63 cm (25 in) [63 cm (25 in): 66 cm (26 in): 66 cm (26 in): 69 cm (27¼ in): 69 cm (27¼ in)]

BACK

RIGHT SLEEVE

44 cm (17¼ in) [44 cm (17¼ in): 47 cm (18½ in): 47 cm (18½ in): 50 cm (19¾ in): 50 cm (19¾ in)]

LEFT SLEEVE

5 cm (2 in)

2 cm (1 in)

FRONT

40 cm (15¾ in) [40 cm (15¾ in): 41 cm (16 in): 41 cm (16 in): 42 cm (16½ in): 42 cm (16½ in)]

48 cm (19 in) [48 cm (19 in): 50 cm (19½ in): 50 cm (19½ in): 52 cm (20¼ in)]

51 cm (20 in) [54 cm (21¼ in): 56 cm (22 in): 59 cm (23¼ in): 61 cm (24 in): 64 cm (25 in)]

WOMAN'S SMOCK SWEATER
CHILD'S SMOCK
COTTON SWEATERS

Shape shoulder

Cast off remaining sts loosely. Return to sts on spare needle. Sl centre st onto a safety pin, rejoin yarn, pattern to end.

Next row. Pattern to end.

Next row. K1, sl 1, K1, psso, pattern to end.

Complete to match first side of neck, reversing shapings.

SLEEVES

With 2¾ mm (no 2) needles, cast on 47 [47:49:49:53:53] sts. Work in rib as given for back for 5 cm, ending with a 1st row.

Next row. Rib 2 [2:1:1:3:3], *inc 1 into next st, rib 1; repeat from * to last 3 [3:2:2:4:4] sts, inc 1 into next st, rib 2 [2:1:1:3:3]. (69 [69:73:73:77:77] sts.)

Change to 3¼ mm (no 3) needles and commence pattern as follows:

1st row. K18[18:20:20:22:22] sts, work from * to * as given for 1st row of back, K to end.

2nd row. P18[18:20:20:22:22] sts, work from * to * as given for 2nd row of back, P to end.

These 2 rows establish position of the cable panel with edge sts in ridge pattern.

Keeping continuity of pattern as given for back, inc 1 st at each end of 7th and every following 6th row until there are 105 [105:113:113:121:121] sts.

Work straight until the sleeve measures 50 cm (19¾ in) [50 cm (19¾ in):52 cm (20¼ in):52 cm (20¼ in):54 cm (21¼ in):54 cm (21¼ in)], ending with a WS row. Cast off loosely.

MAKING UP

Do not press.

Join shoulder seams.

Neckband

With set of four 2¾ mm (no 2) needles, and RS of work facing, K back neck sts, pick up and K68 [68:72:72:76:76] sts from left side of neck, K centre st from safety pin, pick up and K68 [68:72:72:76:76] sts from the right-hand side of neck.

1st round. Work in K1, P1 rib to within 2 sts of centre front st, P2 tog, K1, P2 tog tbl, rib to end.

Repeat this round 6 times more. Cast off in rib, dec as before.

Set in sleeves, sewing last 2 cm (¾ in) of seam to cast-off sts at underarms.

Join side and sleeve seams in one continuous seam.

Woman's Smock Sweater (page 46)

MEASUREMENTS

To fit bust: 86 cm (34 in) [91 cm (36 in):96 cm (38 in)]

Length from shoulder: 64 cm (25½ in) [66.5 cm (26½ in):69 cm (27½ in)]

Sleeve seam: 46 cm (18½ in)

Instructions are given for the smallest size first with larger sizes in the following square brackets.

MATERIALS

650 g (26 oz) [700 g (28 oz):700 g (28 oz)] chunky yarn

Oddments of contrasting double knitting for smocking

1 pair each of 5 mm (no 7) and 6½ mm (no 10) knitting needles

TENSION

14 sts and 18 rows to 10 cm (4 in) over reverse st st on 6½ mm (no 10) needles

BACK

With 6½ mm (no 10) needles, cast on 91 [95:99] sts. Work in moss st as follows:

1st row. K1, *P1, K1; repeat from * to end.

Repeat this row for 4 cm (1½ in) [4 cm (1½ in:5 cm (2 in)]. Now work in reverse st st beg with an RS (P) row, dec 1 st at each end of 7th row and every following 6th row until 73 [77:81] sts remain. Continue without shaping until work measures 43 cm (17 in) [44.5 cm (17½ in):46 cm (18 in)] ending with a K row. Work ribbed panel.

Next row. P19 [21:23], (K1, P1) 17 times, P1, P19 [21:23].

Next row. K19 [21:23], (P1, K1) 17 times, P1, K19 [21:23].

Repeat the last 2 rows until ribbed panel measures 18 cm (7 in) [19 cm (7½ in):20 cm (8 in)], ending with a K row.

Divide for neck

Next row. P19 [21:23], leave these sts on a spare needle, cast of 35 sts, P to end.

Continue on these 19 [21:23] sts for left side of neck. Work straight for 5 rows. Cast off. Rejoin yarn to sts on spare needle.

Work 5 rows. Cast off.

FRONT

Work as given for the back of the sweater.

SLEEVES

Join shoulder seams.

Measure 18 cm (7½ in) [19 cm (7¾ in):20 cm (8 in)] down from shoulder on back and front and mark with pins.

With 6½ mm (no 10) needles, with RS facing, pick up and P63 [67:71] sts between pins.

Continue in reverse st st beg with a WS (K) row, dec 1 st at each end of every following 3rd row until 49 sts remain.

Now work straight until sleeve measures 36 cm (14 in) or required length, ending with a P row.

Next row. *K2, K2 tog; repeat from * to last st, K1. (37 sts).

Continue in K1, P1 rib for 5 cm (2 in), then work in moss st as given for back for 5 cm (2 in). Cast off in moss st.

COLLARS (make 2)

With 5 mm (no 7) needles, cast on 43 sts.

Work in moss st as given for back for 9 cm (3½ in). Cast off in moss st.

MAKING UP

Using contrast yarn smock ribbed panels as shown in diagrams, drawing together alternate pairs of ribs on each smocking row. Work smocking rows about 2.5 cm (1 in) apart. Join side and sleeve seams. Sew on collars.

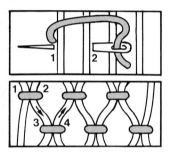

Child's Smock (page 46)

MEASUREMENTS

To fit chest: 51 cm (20 in) [56 cm (22 in:61 cm (24 in)]

Length from shoulder: 36.5 cm (14½ in) [44.5 cm (17½ in):48 cm (19 in)]

Sleeve seam: 17.5 (7 in) [21 cm (8½ in):25 cm (10 in)]

Instructions are given for the smallest size first with larger sizes in the following square brackets.

MATERIALS

175g (7oz) [200g (8oz):200g (8 oz)] superwash double knitting wool

Oddments of contrast yarn for smocking

1 pair each of 3 mm (no 2) and 4½ mm (no 6) knitting needles

TENSION

20 sts to 10 cm (4 in) over reverse st st on 4½ mm (no 6) needles

BACK AND FRONT (one piece)

Begin at lower front edge.

With 4½ mm (no 6) needles, cast on 81 [87:95] sts. Work in moss st as given for back of woman's smock for 5 [6:7] rows. Now work in reverse st st beg with an RS (P) row until front measures 20 cm (8 in) [26.5 cm (10½ in):29 cm (11½ in)], ending with a K row.

Work ribbed panel

Next row. P20 [23:27], (K1, P3) 10 times, K1, P20 [23:27].

Next row. K20 [23:27], (P1, K3) 10 times, P1, K20 [23:27].

Repeat the last 2 rows until ribbed panel measures 11.5 cm (4½ in) [(13 cm (5 in):14 cm (5½ in)], ending with a K row.

Divide for neck

Next row. P20 [23:27], leave these sts on a spare needle, cast off 41 sts, P20 [23:27].

Continue on these sts for right side of neck. Work 13 [15:15] rows in reverse st st. Leave these sts on a spare needle and return to sts on 1st spare needle. Continue on these sts for left side of neck, work 13 [15:15] rows.

Next row. P to end, now cast on 41 sts, P across sts on 2nd spare needle. (81 [87:95] sts).

Now continue in reverse st st and ribbed panel pattern, work back until ribbed panel matches same as front panel. Continue in reverse st st only for 18.5 cm (7¼ in) [24 cm (9½ in):26.5 cm

(10½ in)]. Now work 5 [6:7] rows in moss st. Cast off in moss st.

SLEEVES

Fold front and back piece in half and mark shoulder line on both sides. Measure 10 cm (4 in) [11.5 cm (4½ in):13 cm (5 in)] down from shoulder line on back and front and mark with pins. With 4½ mm (no 6) needles, with RS of work facing, pick up and P60 [70:80] sts between pins. Work in reverse st st, dec 1 st at beginning of every row until 44 [54:64] sts remain.

Now work straight until sleeve measures 11.5 cm (4½ in) [15 cm (6 in):19 cm (7½ in)] or required length, ending with a P row. Change to 3 mm (no 2) needles.

Next row. K8 [3:3], (K2 tog) to last 8 [3:3] sts, K to end. (30 [30:35] sts).

Work in K1, P1 rib for 3.5 cm (1½ in), then work in moss st for 2.5 cm (1 in). Cast off in moss st.

COLLARS (make 2)

With 3 mm (no 2) needles, cast on 45 [49:49] sts. Work moss st for 6 cm (2½ in). Cast off in moss st.

MAKING UP

Using contrast yarn smock ribbed panels as shown in diagrams drawing together alternate pairs of ribs on each smocking row. Work smocking rows about 2 cm (¾ in) apart. Join side and sleeve seams. Sew on collars.

Lacy Sweater (page 51)

MEASUREMENTS

To fit bust: 86-91 cm (34-36 in) [91-96 cm (36-38 in)]
Length from shoulder: 58 cm (23 in) [61 cm (24 in)]
Sleeve seam: 48 cm (19 in)
Instructions are given for the smallest size first with the larger size in the following square brackets.

MATERIALS

400 g (16 oz) [450 g (18 oz)] chunky yarn
1 metre (39 in) of gathered cotton lace, 6 cm (2½ in) wide
1 pair each of 4½ mm (no 6) and 5½ mm (no 8) knitting needles

TENSION

16 sts and 20 rows to 10 cm (4 in) over pattern on 5½ mm (no 8) needles

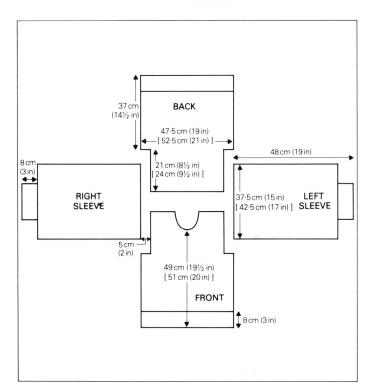

BACK

With 4½ mm (no 6) needles, cast on 75 [83] sts.

Work in K1, P1 rib for 8 cm (3 in), ending with a WS row, inc 1 st at end of last row. (76 [84] sts.) Change to 5½ mm (no 8) needles and continue in pattern as follows:

1st row. (RS) K2, *yfwd, K1 tbl, yfwd, sl 1, K1, psso, K5; repeat from * to last 2 sts, K2.
2nd row. P6, *P2 tog tbl, P7; repeat from * to last 7 sts, P2 tog tbl, P5.
3rd row. K2, *yfwd, K1 tbl, yfwd, K2, sl 1, K1, psso, K3; repeat from * to last 2 sts, K2.
4th row. P4, *P2 tog tbl, P7; repeat from * to end.
5th row. K2, *K1 tbl, yfwd, K4, sl 1, K1, psso, K1, yfwd; repeat from * to last 2 sts, K2.
6th row. P3, *P2 tog tbl, P7; repeat from * to last st, P1.
7th row. K2, *K5, K2 tog, yfwd, K1 tbl, yfwd; repeat from * to last 2 sts, K2.
8th row. P5, *P2 tog, P7; repeat from * to last 8 sts, P2 tog, P6.
9th row. K2, *K3, K2 tog, K2, yfwd, K1 tbl, yfwd; repeat from * to last 2 sts, K2.
10th row. *P7, P2 tog; repeat from * to last 4 sts, P4.
11th row. K2, *yfwd, K1, K2 tog, K4, yfwd, K1 tbl; repeat from * to last 2 sts, K2.
12th row. P1, *P7, P2 tog; repeat from * to last 3 sts, P3.

These 12 rows form the pattern repeat. Continue in pattern until work measures 37 cm (14½ in) [38 cm (15 in)], ending with a WS row.

Shape armholes

Keeping pattern correct, cast off 8 sts at beg of next row and 9 sts at beg of following row. (60 [68] sts.)**

Work straight until the work measures 58 cm (23 in) [61 cm (24 in)], ending with a WS row.

Shape shoulders

Next row. Cast off 18 [22] sts, pattern to end.
Next row. Cast off 18 [22] sts plus extra made sts, then pattern to end.
Leave remaining sts on a spare needle.

FRONT

Work as given for back to **
Work straight until the front measures 49 cm (19½ in) [51 cm (20 in)], ending with a WS row.

Shape neck

Keeping the pattern correct, pattern 26 [30] sts, turn, leaving remaining sts on a spare needle. Work 2 rows.

Cast off 9 sts at beg of next row. 18 [22] sts.

Work straight until the front matches back to shoulder, ending with a WS row.

Shape shoulder

Cast off remaining sts.

Return to sts on spare needle. Sl centre 8 sts onto a stitch holder, rejoin yarn and pattern to end. Work 1 row.

Cast off 8 sts at beg of next row. Now complete to match first side of neck.

SLEEVES

With 4½ mm (no 6) needles, cast on 41 [47] sts.

Work in K1, P1 rib for 8 cm (3 in), ending with a RS row.

Next row. Rib 2 [3], *inc 1 into next st, rib 1; repeat from * to last 1 [2] sts, rib 1 [2]. (60 [68] sts.)

Change to 5½ mm (no 8) needles and continue in pattern as given for back until the work measures 48 cm (19 in), ending with a WS row.

Place marker at each end of last row.

Work a further 5 cm (2 in) in pattern.

Cast off loosely.

MAKING UP

Join left shoulder seam.

Neckband

With 4½ mm (no 6) needles, with RS of work facing, K back neck sts, inc 7 sts evenly across them, pick up and K19 [21] sts from left side of neck, K front neck sts, then pick up and K19 [21] sts from right side of neck. (77 [81] sts.)

Next row. P1, *K1, P1; repeat from * to end.

Next row. K1, *P1, K1; repeat from * to end.

Repeat the last 2 rows twice more.

Cast off in rib.

Join right shoulder seam and neckband.

Sew in sleeves, joining the last rows to cast-off sts at underarms. Join side and sleeve seams. Sew gathered edge of lace inside neckband, joining ends at the shoulder seam.

MULTICOLOURED SWEATER
BOBBLE SWEATER
LACY SWEATER

Multicoloured Sweater (page 50)

Soft fluffy yarn in five different colours make up this richly textured sweater. In spite of its complicated appearance, the stitches used are garter stitch, stocking stitch and simple colourwork and bobbles, which should not be too difficult even for beginners.

MEASUREMENTS

To fit bust: 81-86 cm (32-34 in) [86-91 cm (34-36 in):91-96 cm (36-38 in)]
Length from shoulder: 63 cm (24¾ in) [64 cm (25 in):65 cm (25½ in)]
Sleeve seam: 43 cm (17 in)
Instructions are given for the smallest size first with larger sizes in the following square brackets.

MATERIALS

200 g (8 oz) [225 g (9 oz):250 g (10 oz)] mohair type yarn in main colour (A)
50 g mohair type yarn in 1st contrast colour (B)
75g (3 oz) [75 g (3 oz):100g (4 oz)] mohair in 2nd contrast (C)
50 g (2 oz) [50 g (2 oz):75 g (3 oz)] double knitting in each of 3rd and 4th contrast colours (D and E)
1 pair each of 3¼ mm (no 3), 4 mm (no 5), 4½ mm (no 6) and 5½ mm (no 8) knitting needles

TENSION

22 sts and 30 rows to 10 cm (4 in) over st st on 4 mm (no 5) needles
16 sts and 21 rows to 10 cm (4 in) over st st on 5½ mm (no 8) needles

EXTRA ABBREVIATIONS

MB – make bobble: K into front, back, front and back of next st, making 4 sts, turn, K4, turn, P4, turn, (K2 tog) twice, turn, P2 tog.

BACK

With 4½ mm (no 6) needles and A, cast on 74 [78:82] sts.
1st row. K2, *P2, K2; repeat from * to end.
2nd row. P2, *K2, P2; repeat from * to end.
Repeat these 2 rows 5 times more, then the last row again.
Next row. Rib 9, (inc 1 into next st, rib 1) 28 [30:32] times, inc 1 into next st; rib 8. (103 [109:115] sts.)
Continue in pattern as follows:

Change to 3¼ mm (no 3) needles and D. Work 4 rows g st. Change to 4 mm (no 5) needles and E. Beg with a K row work 4 rows st st.
9th row. K1C, *5B, 1C; repeat from * to end.
10th row. P2C, *3B, 3C; repeat from * to last 5 sts, 3B, 2C.
11th row. K1B, *2C, 1B; repeat from * to end.
12th row. P2B, *3C, 3B; repeat from * to last 5 sts, 3C, 2B.
13th row. K3B, *1C, 5B; repeat from * to last 4 sts, 1C, 3B.
With E, beg with a P row, work 5 rows st st.
Change to 3¼ mm (no 3) needles and D. Work 4 rows g st. Change to 4 mm (no 5) needles.
23rd row. K3A, *1E, 5A; repeat from * to last 4 sts, 1E, 3A.
24th row. P2A, *3E, 3A; repeat from * to last 5 sts, 3E, 2A.
25th row. K1A, *5E, 1A; repeat from * to end.
26th row. With E, P.
27th row. K3E, *MB in A, K5E; repeat from * to last 4 sts, MB in A, K3E.
28th row. P1A, *5E, 1A; repeat from * to end.
29th row. K2A, *3E, 3A; repeat from * to last 5 sts, 3E, 2A.
30th row. P3A, *1E, 5A; repeat from * to last 4 sts, 1E, 3A.
Change to 3¼ mm (no 3) needles and D. Work 4 rows g st. Change to 4 mm (no 5) needles and repeat 23rd-30th rows but using C instead of A and D instead of E.
The last 42 rows form the pattern repeat. Continue in pattern until work measures 43 cm (17 in), ending with a WS row.
Shape armholes
Keeping pattern correct, cast off 5 [6:7] sts at beg of next 2 rows. Dec 1 st at each end of next 3 rows and following 3 alt rows. (81 [85:89] sts.)
Work straight until the work measures 63 cm (24¾ in) [64 cm (25 in):65 cm (25½ in)], ending with a WS row.
Shape shoulders
Cast off 9 sts at beg of next 4 rows and 8 [9:10] sts at beg of following 2 rows. Leave remaining 29 [31:33] sts on a spare needle.

FRONT

Work as given for back until work measures 57 cm (22½ in) [58 cm (23 in):59 cm (23¼ in)], ending with a WS row.
Shape neck
Next row. Pattern 31 [32:33] sts, turn, leaving remaining sts on a spare needle.
Dec 1 st at neck edge on next 5 rows. (26 [27:28] sts.)
Work straight until the front matches back to shoulder, ending with a WS row.
Shape shoulder
Cast off 9 sts at beg of next and following alt row. Work 1 row. Cast off remaining 8 [9:10] sts.
Return to sts on spare needle, sl centre 19 [21:23] sts onto a stitch holder, rejoin yarn and pattern to end. Complete to match first side reversing shapings.

SLEEVES

With 4½ mm (no 6) needles and A, cast on 30 [34:38] sts. Work 14 rows K2, P2 rib as given for back, inc 9 sts evenly across last row. (39 [43:47] sts.)
Change to 5½ mm (no 8) needles and continue in st st. Inc 1 st at each end of 11th and every following 6th row until there are 61 [65:69] sts.
Work straight until the sleeve measures 43 cm (17 in), ending with a P row.
Shape top
Cast off 4 [5:6] sts at beg of next 2 rows.
Dec 1 st at each end of next and every following alt row until 37 sts remain, ending with a P row. Cast off 2 sts at beg of next 4 rows. Cast off remaining 29 sts.

MAKING UP

Join left shoulder seam.
Neckband
With 4½ mm (no 6) needles and A, with RS of work facing, K across back neck sts, dec 5 sts evenly across them, pick up and K17 [19:21] sts from left side of neck, K front neck sts, dec 3 sts evenly across them, pick up and K17 [19:21] sts from right side of neck. (74 [82:90] sts.)
Beg with a 2nd row, work 14 rows rib as given for back. Cast off in rib.
Join right shoulder and neckband seam. Set in sleeves. Join side and sleeve seams. Fold neckband in half to WS and slipstitch down.

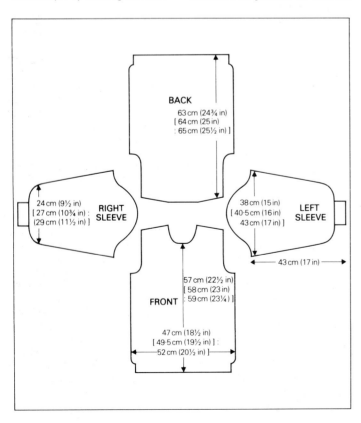

BACK
63 cm (24¾ in)
[64 cm (25 in)
: 65 cm (25½ in)]

24 cm (9½ in)
[27 cm (10¾ in) :
(29 cm (11½ in)
RIGHT SLEEVE

38 cm (15 in)
[40·5 cm (16 in)
43 cm (17 in)]
LEFT SLEEVE

43 cm (17 in)

FRONT
57 cm (22½ in)
[58 cm (23 in)
: 59 cm (23¼ in)]

47 cm (18½ in)
[49·5 cm (19½ in)] :
52 cm (20½ in)]

Bobble Sweater (page 51)

MEASUREMENTS
To fit bust: 81 cm (32 in) [86 cm (34 in):91 cm (36 in)]
Length from shoulder: 54 cm (21¼ in) [57 cm (22½ in):60 cm (23¾ in)]
Sleeve seam: 44 cm (17½ in) [46 cm (18 in):48 cm (19 in)]
Instructions are given for the smallest size first with larger sizes in the following square brackets.

MATERIALS
750 g (30 oz) [850 g (34 oz):1000 g (40 oz)] double knitting yarn
3 buttons
1 pair each of 4 mm (no 5) and 3¼ mm (no 3) knitting needles

TENSION
20 sts and 26 rows to 10 cm (4 in) over st st on 4 mm (no 5) needles

EXTRA ABBREVIATION
MB – make bobble: K into front, back, front, back, then front again of next st, making 5 sts, K next st, turn, P5, turn, K5, turn, P5, turn, sl 2nd, 3rd, 4th and 5th sts over 1st st, then K tbl 1st st.

BACK
With 3¼ mm (no 3) needles, cast on 85 [91:97] sts.
1st row. K2, *P1, K1; repeat from * to last st, K1.
2nd row. K1, *P1, K1; repeat from * to end.
Repeat these 2 rows 7 times more, inc 1 st at end of last row. (86 [92:98] sts.)
Change to 4 mm (no 5) needles and pattern as follows:
1st row. K4 [7:10], MB, *K13, MB; repeat from * to last 5 [8:11] sts, K to end.
2nd row. K1, P2 [5:8], K5, *P10, K5; repeat from * to last 3 [6:9] sts, P to last st, K1.
3rd row. K to end.
4th row. As 2nd row.
5th-8th rows. As 1st-4th rows.
9th-11th rows. As 1st-3rd rows.
12th row. K.
13th-16th rows. As 1st-4th rows.
17th row. *K1, MB; repeat from * to last 2 sts, K2.
18th row. As 2nd row.
19th and 20th rows. K.
These 20 rows form the pattern repeat. Continue in pattern until work measures 37 cm (14½ in) [39 cm (15½ in):41 cm (16 in)], ending with a WS row.

Shape armholes
Keeping pattern correct, cast off 4 sts at beg of next 2 rows. Dec 1 st at each end of every row until 66 [70:72] sts remain. Work straight until work measures 54 cm (21½ in) [57 cm (22½ in):60 cm 1(23¾ in)], ending with a WS row.

Shape shoulders
Cast off 6 [7:7] sts beg of next 4 rows and 7 sts at beg of next 2 rows. Leave remaining 28 [28:30] sts on a spare needle.

FRONT
Work as for back until work measures approx 30 cm (12 in), ending with 20th pattern row.

Divide for neck
Next row. Pattern 37 [40:43] sts, turn, leaving remaining sts on a spare needle. Work straight until front matches back to armhole, ending at side edge.

Shape armhole
Cast off 4 sts at beg of next row. Work 1 row. Dec 1 st at armhole edge on every following row until 27 [29:30] sts remain. Work straight until front measures 45 cm (17¾ in) [48 cm (19 in):51 cm (20 in)] end with a WS row.

Shape neck
Dec 1 st at neck edge on next 3 rows, then on every alt row until 19 [21:21] sts remain.
Work straight until the front matches back to shoulder, ending at armhole edge.

Shape shoulder
Cast off 6 [7:7] sts at beg of next and following alt row. Work 1 row. Cast off remaining 7 sts. Return to sts on spare needle. Sl centre 12 sts onto a stitch holder, rejoin yarn, pattern to end. Complete to match first side of neck, reversing shapings.

SLEEVES
With 3¼ mm (no 3) needles, cast on 45 [45:49] sts.
Work 22 rows rib as given for back, inc 1 st at each end of last row on 1st and 2nd sizes and inc 4 sts evenly across last row on 3rd size. (47 [47:53] sts.)
Change to 4 mm (no 5) needles. Commence pattern as follows:
1st row. K7 [7:10], MB, *K13, MB; repeat from * to last 8 [8:11] sts, K to end.
2nd row. K1, P5 [5:8], K5, *P10, K5; repeat from * to last 6 [6:9] sts, P to last st, K1.
3rd row. K.

4th row. As 2nd row.
5th-8th rows. As 1st-4th rows.
These 8 rows establish the pattern as given for back. Continue in pattern, inc 1 st at each end of next and every following 8th row until there are 63 [67:71] sts. Work straight until the sleeve measures 44 cm (17½ in) [46 cm (18 in):48 cm (19 in)], ending with a WS row.

Shape top
Keeping pattern correct, cast off 4 sts at beg of next 2 rows. Dec 1 st at each end of next and every following alt row until 35 [39:43] sts remain. Work 1 row. Dec 1 st at each end of every row until 15 sts remain. Cast off.

MAKING UP
Join shoulder seams.

Borders
With 3¼ mm (no 3) needles, cast on 1 st, then K first 3 sts from stitch holder at centre front, turn, cast on 6 sts. (10 sts.)
Continue in g st until border fits front opening edge to neck shaping, ending with a WS row. Leave sts on a spare needle. Break yarn.
Mark the position of 3 buttons, the first 5 cm (2 in) from lower edge, the last 3 cm (1¼ in) from upper edge, with the other evenly spaced between. With 3¼ mm (no 3) needles, K9 sts from centre front stitch holder, cast on 1 st. (10 sts.)
Continue in g st until border fits front opening edge to neck shaping, ending with a WS row, *at the same time*, making buttonholes opposite markers as follows:
1st row. (RS) K3, cast off 2, K to end.
2nd row. K to end, casting on 2 sts over those cast off in previous row.

Collar
With 3¼ mm needles, K10 sts of right front border, pick up and K25 [25:27] sts from right side of neck, K back neck sts, pick up and K25 [25:27] sts from left side of neck, K10 sts of left front border. (98 [98:104] sts.)
Work 11 cm (4½ in) [11 cm (4½ in):12 cm (4¾ in)] g st, end with a RS row of collar. Cast off.
Join side and sleeve seams. Set in sleeves. Sew borders to edges of opening, catching right front over left at base.
Sew on buttons.

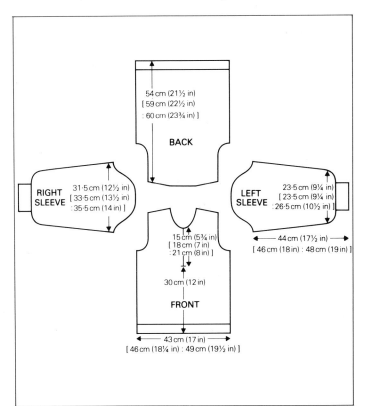

BACK
54 cm (21½ in) [59 cm (22½ in) : 60 cm (23¾ in)]

RIGHT SLEEVE
31·5 cm (12½ in) [33·5 cm (13½ in) : 35·5 cm (14 in)]

LEFT SLEEVE
23·5 cm (9¼ in) [23·5 cm (9¼ in) : 26·5 cm (10½ in)]

44 cm (17½ in) [46 cm (18 in) : 48 cm (19 in)]

15 cm (5¾ in) [18 cm (7 in) : 21 cm (8 in)]

30 cm (12 in)

FRONT
43 cm (17 in) [46 cm (18¼ in) : 49 cm (19½ in)]

GARTER STITCH BABY OUTFIT
BATWING SWEATER

Garter Stitch Baby Outfit (page 54)

MEASUREMENTS
Age: 6-9 months
To fit chest: 50 cm (20 in)
Length from shoulder: 24 cm (9½ in)

MATERIALS
Pullover
50 g (2 oz) 4-ply baby yarn in each of 3 colours (A, B, C)

Bootees and bonnet
50 g (2 oz) 4-ply baby yarn in each of 3 colours
1 pair each of 2¼ mm (no 0) and 2¾ mm (no 1) knitting needles
Ribbon (for bootees)

TENSION
26 sts and 48 rows to 10 cm (4 in) over g st on 2¾ mm (no 1) needles

BACK AND FRONT (one piece)
With 2¼ mm (no 0) needles and C, cast on 66 sts. Work in g st for 6 rows.
Change to 2¾ mm (no 1) needles. Continue in g st, work 6 rows in A, 6 rows in B, then 6 rows in C. Continue working g st stripes in this sequence until 60 rows have been worked in all.
Change to A and continue in g st for 24 rows.
Divide for neck
Next row. K33, turn, leaving remaining sts on a spare needle. K 8 rows.
Shape neck
Next row. Cast off 10 sts, K to end. (23 sts)

K 19 rows. Break yarn. Leave remaining sts on a spare needle. Rejoin yarn to inner edge of sts on first spare needle. K 8 rows.
Shape neck
Next row. Cast off 10 sts, K to end. (23 sts)
K 19 rows. Now join both sides of neck for back as follows:
Next row. Cast on 20 sts, K to end. (43 sts)
Next row. K43. Then K across 23 sts left on second spare needle. (66 sts)
Continue in g st for 52 rows.
Now work in g st stripes, work 6 rows in C, 6 rows in B and 6 rows in A. Repeat the last 18 rows twice more.
Change to 2¼ mm (no 0) needles and C.
K 6 rows. Cast off loosely.

SLEEVES
With 2¼ mm (no 0) needles and A cast on 58 sts. K 6 rows.
Change to 2¾ mm (no 1) needles. Continue in g st, work 6 rows in B, then 6 rows in C.
Change to A and continue in g st until work measures 15 cm (6 in). Cast off loosely.

MAKING UP
Set in sleeves flat, positioning cast-off edge of sleeve between stripes on front and back.
Join side and sleeve seams.

BOOTEES (both alike)
With 2¼ mm (no 0) needles and B, cast on 34 sts. K 6 rows.
Change to 2¾ mm (no 1) needles and K 6 rows in A and 6 rows in C.
Continue in B, make eyelets as follows:
Next row. K1, *yfwd, K2 tog; repeat from * to last st, K1.
Next row. K to end.
Divide for foot
Next row. K23, turn.
Next row. K12, turn.
Continue on these 12 sts only, K 16 rows. Break yarn. With RS of work facing pick up and K11 up right side of foot, K across 12 sts on LH needle, dec 1 st in centre by K2 tog, then pick up and K11 down left side of foot, K11 from LH needle. (55 sts)
Continue in g st, work 11 rows.
Shape toe
Next row. *K1, K2 tog, K22, K2 tog; repeat from * to last st, K1.
Next row. K.
Next row. *K1, K2 tog, K20, K2 tog; repeat from * to last st, K1.
Next row. K.
Next row. *K1, K2 tog, K18, K2 tog; repeat from * to last st, K1.
Cast off remaining sts.

MAKING UP
Join seam.
Thread a length of ribbon through the eyelet holes at the ankles and tie in bow.

BONNET
With 2¼ mm (no 0) needles and B, cast on 188 sts. K 6 rows.
Cast off 50 sts at beg of next 2 rows. (88 sts)
Change to 2¾ mm (no 1) needles and continue in g st stripes sequence, work 6 rows in A, 6 rows in C, 6 rows in B, for 42 rows.
Shape crown
Keep stripe pattern correct.
Next row. K10, K2 tog, (K11, K2 tog) twice, K12, K2 tog, (K11, K2 tog) twice, K10. (82 sts)
2nd and every alt row. K.
3rd row. (K10, K2 tog) 6 times, K10. (76 sts)
5th row. K10, K2 tog, (K9, K2 tog) twice, K8, K2 tog, (K9, K2 tog) twice, K10. (70 sts)
7th row. K10, K2 tog, (K8, K2 tog) twice, K6, K2 tog, (K8, K2 tog) twice, K10. (64 sts)
9th row. K10, K2 tog, (K7, K2 tog) twice, K4, K2 tog, (K7, K2 tog) twice, K10. (58 sts)
11th row. K10, K2 tog, (K6, K2 tog) twice, K2, K2 tog, (K6, K2 tog) twice, K10. (52 sts)
13th row. K10, K2 tog, (K5, K2 tog) twice, K2 tog, (K5, K2 tog) twice, K10. (46 sts)
15th row. (K2 tog) to end. (23 sts)
17th row. (K2 tog) to last st, K1. (12 sts)
Break yarn and thread it through remaining stitches, draw up tightly and fasten off securely on wrong side.

MAKING UP
Join back seam to within 5 cm (2 in) of beginning of straps.

Batwing Sweater (page 55)

MEASUREMENTS
Age: 6 [7:8] years
To fit chest: 60 cm (24 in) [62 cm (25 in):64 cm (26 in)]
Actual width measurement: 74 cm (29½ in) [76 cm (30½ in):78 cm (31½ in)]
Length at centre back: 40.5 cm (16 in) [42 cm (17 in):44.5 cm (18 in)]
Sleeve seam: 32 cm (13 in) [34 cm (13½ in):35 cm (14 in)]
Instructions are given for the smallest size first with larger sizes in the following square brackets.

MATERIALS
250 g (10 oz) [300 g (12 oz):300 g (12 oz)] fluffy wool/acrylic yarn (A)
25 g (1 oz) metallic/acrylic yarn (B)
1 pair each of 3¼ mm (no 3) and 4 mm (no 5) knitting needles

TENSION
18 sts and 26 rows to 10 cm (4 in) over st st on 4 mm (no 5) needles

BACK
With 3¼ mm (no 3) needles and A, cast on 60 [64:64] sts. Work in K2, P2 rib for 5 cm (2 in).

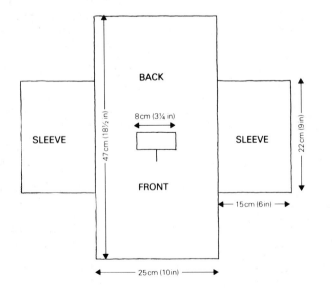

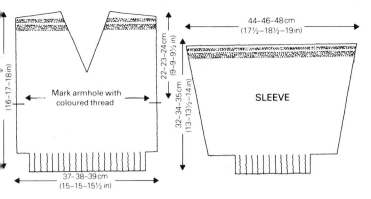

Mark armhole with coloured thread

(16-17-18 in)

22-23-24 cm (9-9-9½ in)

32-34-35 cm (13-13½-14 in)

37-38-39 cm (15-15-15½ in)

44-46-48 cm (17½-18½-19 in)

SLEEVE

Next row. Rib 6 [8:7], M1, (rib 7 [9:7] sts, M1) 7 [5:7] times, rib to end. (68 [70:72] sts)

Change to 4 mm (no 5) needles and continue in st st until work measures 18 cm (7 in) [19 cm (7½ in):20 cm (8 in)] ending with a P row.

Mark each end of last row with coloured thread for armholes. Continue in st st for a further 48 [52:56] rows.

Change to B (use double if necessary) and work stripe pattern as follows:

1st-4th rows. Work in st st in B.
5th-6th rows. Work in st st in A.
7th-8th rows. Work in st st in B.
9th-10th rows. Work in st st in A.

Shape shoulders

With A, cast off 8 sts at beg of next 6 rows. (20 [22:24] sts)

Sl remaining sts onto a stitch holder.

FRONT

Work as given for back to armhole markers. Continue in st st for 30 [32:32] rows.

Divide for neck

Next row. K34 [35:36], turn, leaving remaining sts on spare needle.

Continue on these sts only for right side of neck.

Next row. P to end.

Continue in st st, dec 1 st at neck edge on next and following 6 [7:7] alt rows. Now dec 1 st on every following 4th row 3 [3:4] times *at the same time* work stripe pattern as given for back, beg on 49th [53rd:57th] row from armhole markers.

Shape shoulder

Cast off 8 sts at beg of next and following alt row. Work 1 row. Cast off remaining 8 sts.

Rejoin yarn to sts on spare needle and continue on these for right side of neck.

Next row. K.

Complete to match left side of neck reversing shapings.

SLEEVES

With 3¼ mm (no 3) needles and A, cast on 28 [32:32] sts. Work in K2, P2 rib until work measures 5 cm (2 in).

Next row. (Rib 1, inc 1) to end. (56 [64:64] sts)

Change to 4 mm (no 5) needles and work in st st, inc 1 st at each end of every following 5th row 11 [6:4] times. Now inc 1 st at each end of every following 6th row 0 [5:7] times. 78 [82:86] sts)

Work straight until 60 [66:68] rows have been worked from top of rib. Now work stripe pattern as given for back.

Cast off.

MAKING UP

Join right shoulder seam.

Neckband

With 3¼ mm (no 3) needles and A, with RS of work facing, pick up and K31 [35:39] sts down left side of neck, 31 [35:39] sts up right side of neck, K across 20 [22:24] sts from stitch holder at back neck, inc 2 sts evenly on 1st and 3rd sizes only. 84 [92:104] sts.

Work in K2, P2 rib as follows:

1st row. (K2, P2) to end.
2nd row. Rib to within 4 sts of centre front, sl 2, P1, p2sso K2, P3 tog, rib to end.

Repeat last 2 rows twice more. Cast off loosely in rib.

Join left shoulder seam and neckband. Set in sleeves between markers.

Join sleeve and side seams.

Striped Raglan Sweater (page 58)

MEASUREMENTS

To fit chest: 56 cm (22 in) [58 cm (23 in):60 cm (24 in)]

Width at underarm: 60 cm (24 in) [64 cm (25½ in):68 cm (27 in)]

Centre back length: 40 cm (16 in) [41 cm (16½ in):42.5 cm (17 in)]

Sleeve seam excluding cuff: 30 cm (12 in) [31 cm (12½ in): 32 cm (13 in)]

Instructions are given for the smallest size first with larger sizes in the following square brackets.

MATERIALS

Striped version (all sizes)

100 g (4 oz) double knitting wool/nylon mixture in main colour (A)

50 g (2 oz) in each of 3 contrast colours (B, C, D)

Plain version (all sizes)

300 g (6 oz) in 1 colour only

1 pair each of 3¾ mm (no 4) and 4 mm (no 5) knitting needles

TENSION

22 sts and 30 rows to 10 cm (4 in) over st st on 4 mm (no 5) needles

BACK

With 3¾ mm (no 4) needles and A, cast on 60 [64:68] sts. Work 17 rows in K1, P1 rib.

Next row. Rib 10 [10:9], *M1, rib 8 [9:10]; repeat from * to last 10 [9:9] sts, M1, rib to end. (66 (70:74] sts)

Change to 4 mm (no 5) needles and work in st st stripes as follows:

1st-6th rows. Work in st st in B.
7th-12th rows. Work in st st in C.
13th-18th rows. Work st st in D.
19th-24th rows. Work st st in A.

Repeat these 24 rows until 62 [64:66] rows in all have been worked in stripe pattern.

Shape raglan armholes

Keeping pattern correct cast off 2 sts at beg of next 2 rows. Work 2 rows straight.

Next row. K2, K2 tog tbl, K to last 4 sts, K2 tog, K2.

Next row. P**.

Repeat the last 2 rows until 24 [26:28] sts remain, ending with a P row. Sl remaining sts onto a stitch holder.

FRONT

Work as for back to **. Repeat the last 2 rows until 34 [36:38] sts remain, ending with a P row.

Divide for neck

Next row. K2, K2 tog tbl, K9 [10:11], turn, leaving remaining sts on spare needle.

Continue on these sts only for left side of neck. Dec 1 st at neck edge on next 6 [7:8] rows *at the same time* dec at raglan edge as before until 2 sts remain. K2 tog and fasten off.

Return to sts on spare needle. With RS of work facing sl next 8 sts onto a stitch holder, rejoin yarn to next st, work to end of row. Keeping stripe pattern correct complete to match left side, reversing shapings.

SLEEVES

With 3¾ mm (no 4) needles and A, cast on 32 [34:36] sts. Work 36 rows in K1, P1 rib. Change to 4 mm (no 5) needles. Beg with 13th row of pattern work in stripe pattern as given for back, inc 1 st each end of every following 8th row until there are 48 [50:52] sts, ending with a P row. Work 10 [12:14] rows straight.

Shape raglan armholes

Keeping pattern correct cast off 2 sts at beg of next 2 rows. Work 2 rows straight. Now working dec rows as given for back dec 1 st at each end of every alt row until 6 sts remain. Work 1 row. Sl remaining sts onto a safety pin.

MAKING UP

Press according to instructions on ball band. Join raglan seams leaving right back open.

Neckband

With RS of work facing, with 3¾ mm (no 4) needles and A, K across back neck sts as follows: K3 [4:5], M1, (K3, M1) 6 times, K3 [4:5]; now K6 sts from left sleeve, pick up and K10 [10:11] sts down left side of neck, K8 sts from stitch holder at front neck, inc 1 st in centre, pick up and K10 [10:11] sts up right side of neck, K6 sts from right sleeve. (72 [74:78] sts)

Work in K1, P1 rib for 2.5 cm (1 in). Cast off loosely in rib. Join right back raglan seam and neck border. Join side and sleeve seams.

21·5–22–23cm
(8½–9–9½ in)

SLEEVE

24–25–26cm
(9½–10–10½ in)

12cm
(5in)

14–14·5–15cm
(5½–5¾–6in)

BACK & FRONT

34–35–36·5cm
(13½–14–14½ in)

6cm
(2½ in)

30–32–34cm
(12–13–13½ in)

STRIPED RAGLAN SWEATER
CHILDREN'S PICTURE DRESSES

Children's Picture Dresses (page 59)

MEASUREMENTS
To fit chest: 56 cm (22 in)
Length from shoulder: 44 cm (17½ in)
Sleeve seam: 34 cm (13½ in)

MATERIALS
Elephant dress
150 g (6 oz) superwash double knitting wool in main colour (A)
50 g (2 oz) in 1st and 2nd contrast colours (B and C)
25 g (1 oz) in 3rd contrast colour (D)
Oddment in 4th contrast colour (E)

Giraffe dress
175 g (7 oz) in main colour (F)
25 g (1 oz) in 1st, 2nd, 3rd and 4th contrast colours (G, H, J, L)
1 pair each of 3¼ mm (no 3) and 4 mm (no 5) knitting needles
4 small buttons (for each dress)

TENSION
22 sts and 28 rows to 10 cm (4 in) over st st on 4 mm (no 5) needles

ELEPHANT DRESS
BACK
With 3¼ mm (no 3) needles and A, cast on 100 sts. Work in st st, beginning with a K row, for 9 rows.
Next row. (WS) K to end. (hemline)
Change to 4 mm (no 5) needles. Work 6 rows in st st, beginning with a K row.
**Next row. With C, K.
Next row. With A, P.
Next row. With A, K.
Next row. With B, K.
Work 5 rows st st, beg with a K row.**
Now commence Fair Isle pattern from chart 1 thus:
1st row. K1A, 1C, *(1A, 1C) twice, 3A, 1C; repeat from * to last 2 sts, 1A, 1C.
2nd row. P1C, 1A, *5A, 1C 1A, 1C; repeat from * to last 2 sts, 1A, 1C.
These 2 rows set the pattern. Now work next 5 rows from chart 1.***
Continue in A only and st st, dec 1 st at each end of the next and every following 8th row until 84 sts remain. Now work straight until back measures 33cm (13in) ending with a P row.

Decrease for yoke
Next row. K11, *K2 tog, K1; repeat from * to last 13 sts, K2 tog, K11. (63 sts)
Next row. P to end.
Now work in Fair Isle pattern from chart 2, at the same time shape armholes thus:
1st row. K9A, K2C, *1A, 2C, 3B, 2C; repeat from * to last 12 sts, K1A, 2C, 9A.
2nd row. With A cast off 8 sts, cast off next st with B, P2C, *1C, 5B, 2C; repeat from * to last 11 sts, 1C, 1B, 9A. (54 sts)
These 2 rows set the Fair Isle pattern. Now continue working from chart, cast off 9 sts in A at beg of next row. (45 sts)
Work straight until work measures 14 cm (5½ in) from armhole, ending with a P row.
Cast off 10 sts, place wool marker on 10th st to mark shoulder, cast off 25 sts, place marker on last st, cast off remaining sts.

FRONT
Work as given for back to ***.
Continue in A only and st st, dec 1 st at each end of next row, then work 6 more rows. (98 sts).
Now work elephant motif from chart 3 thus:
Next row. P36A, 2E, 2A, 1E, 2A, 1E, 9A, 5E, 3A, 1E, 36A.
Next row. K35A, 1E, 1B, 1E, 2A, 1E, 1D, 1E, 1D, 1E, 8A, 1E, 1D, 1A, 2C, 1E, 1A, 2D, 1A, 2E, 33A.
These 2 rows set the position of the motif. Continue to work motif from chart at the same time dec as for back, then continue in A only as for back, dec for yoke and work Fair Isle pattern from chart 2 until yoke measures 11 cm (4¼ in) from beg of armhole ending with a P row.
Shape neck
Next row. K14, leave these sts on a spare needle, cast off 17 sts, K to end. (14 sts)
Continue on these sts only for right side of neck, keeping yoke pattern correct, dec 1 st at neck edge on next 4 rows. Work straight until front matches back to shoulder. Cast off. Return to sts on spare needle. Rejoin yarn to inner edge and complete to match right side of neck.

SLEEVES
With 3¼ mm (no 3) needles and A, cast on 38 sts and work 6 cm (2½ in) in K2, P2 rib. Change to 4 mm (no 5) needles.
Next row. K6, K twice into every st, to last 6 sts, K6. (64 sts)
Now work in st st with A, for 5 rows, beg with a P row. Then work stripe pattern as given for back from ** to **.
Now work pattern from chart 1, working basic pattern repeat only. When chart is complete continue in st st and A until sleeve measures 27 cm (10½ in), ending with a P row, then work 1 row in C, 2 rows in A, 1 row in B, 2 rows in A, 1 row in D, then 13 rows in A. Cast off.

BACK NECKBAND
With 3¼ mm (no 3) needles and A, with RS of work facing, pick up and K24 sts from back neck between shoulder markers. Work 4 cm (1½ in) in K2, P2 rib. Cast off loosely in rib. Fold neckband in half onto WS and slipstitch down.

Chart 1

Chart 2

repeat

repeat

Chart 3

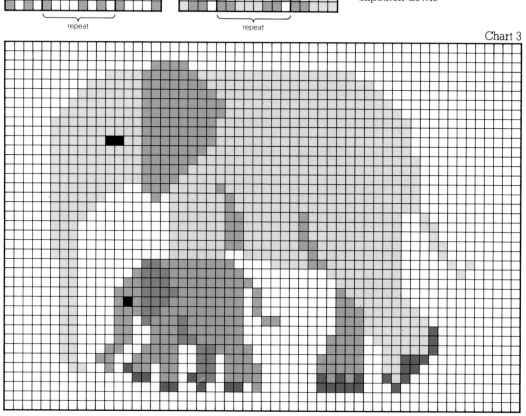

FRONT NECKBAND

With 3¼ mm (no 3) needles and A, with RS of work facing, pick up and K10 sts from left side of neck, 16 sts from front neck and 10 sts up right side of neck. (36 sts)

Work 4 cm (1½ in) in K2, P2 rib.

Cast off loosely in rib. Fold neckband in half onto WS and slipstitch down.

SHOULDER EDGINGS

With 3¼ mm (no 3) needles and A, with RS of work facing and beg at armhole edge pick up

and K10 sts from left front shoulder and 6 sts from top of neckband edge. (16 sts)

Work 5 rows in K2, P2 rib, making buttonholes on 2nd row thus:

Buttonhole row. (Rib 5, yfwd, K2 tog) twice, rib 2. Cast off in rib.

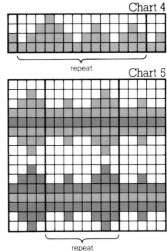

Chart 4

Chart 5

Work right front shoulder edging to match, reversing buttonhole position. Work back shoulder edgings to match front omitting buttonholes.

MAKING UP

Lap front shoulders over back shoulders and sew at armhole edge to secure. Set in sleeves, joining the last 13 rows of st st in A to cast-off sts at armhole. Join side and sleeve seams. Turn up hems on hemline row and slipstitch down. Sew on buttons.

GIRAFFE DRESS
BACK

Work as given for elephant dress using chart 4 (above top) for borders and chart 5 (above) for yoke.

FRONT

Work as given for back until last row of border pattern has been worked. Now work from chart 6 (left) placing motif as follows:

Next row. K45F, 1G, K to end of row in F.

This row sets the position of the chart. Continue working from chart 6 at the same time dec 1 st at each end of every 8th row until 84 sts remain. Complete as given for front of elephant dress, working the yoke pattern from chart 5 (above).

SLEEVES

Work as given for elephant dress using chart 4 (above top) instead of chart 1.

NECKBANDS, SHOULDER EDGINGS AND MAKING UP

Work all these sections as given for the elephant dress using F instead of A.

Chart 6

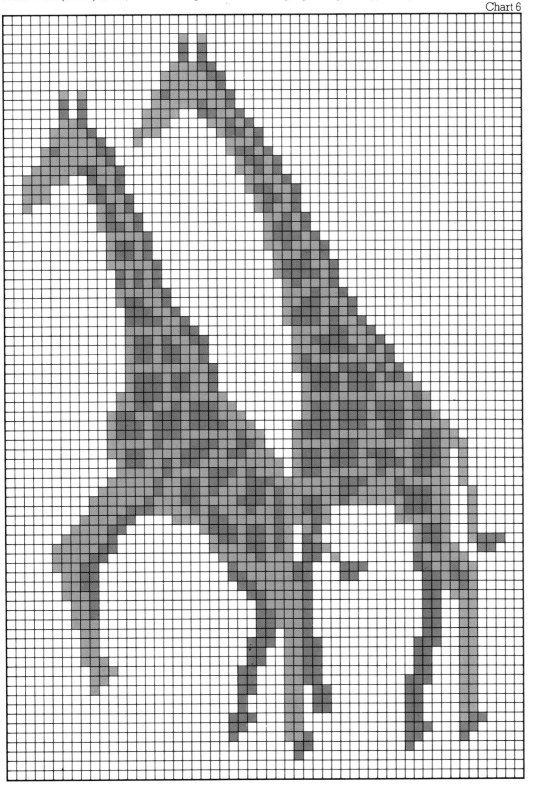

BABY COAT
LACY BABY JACKET

Lacy Baby Jacket (page 62)

Diagram labels: Divide here for armhole · LEFT FRONT · MAIN BODY BACK · RIGHT FRONT · 15–16–18cm (6–6½–7 in) · 58·5–62–62 cm (23½–25–25 in) · Mark here with coloured thread · TOP ARM · SLEEVE · 17–18–19 cm (7–7¼–7½ in) · 18–18–22 cm (7–7–9 in)

MEASUREMENTS
Age: 6 months [12 months:18 months]

To fit chest: 46 cm (18 in) [50 cm (20 in):51 cm (20½ in)]

Length from shoulder: 27 cm (11 in) [28 cm (11 in):29 cm (11½ in)]

Sleeve seam: 15 cm (6 in) [16 cm (6½ in):18 cm (7 in)]

Instructions are given for the smallest size first with larger sizes in the following square brackets.

MATERIALS
150 g (6 oz) 4-ply baby yarn in main colour (A)

50 g (2 oz) in contrast colour (B)

1 pair 2¾ mm (no 1) knitting needles

4 buttons

TENSION
30 sts and 42 rows to 10 cm (4 in) over st st on 2¾ mm (no 1) needles

BACK AND FRONTS (one piece)
With B, cast on 176 [187:187] sts. K3 rows.

Change to A and commence lace pattern.

1st row. (RS) K.

2nd row. P.

3rd row. *(P2 tog) twice, yon, K1, (yfwd, K1) twice, yrn, (P2 tog) twice; repeat from * to end.

4th row. P.

These 4 rows form the lace pattern.

Repeat these 4 rows 11 [12:13] times more.

Divide for armholes
Next row. K44 [46:46], turn, leaving remaining sts on a spare needle.

Continue on these sts only for right front.

Work 2nd-4th rows of lace pattern, now work 1st-4th rows 4 times more.

Next row. (K2 tog) 10[8:2] times, (K1, K2 tog) 7 [9:13] times, K to end. (27 [29:31] sts)

Break yarn and sl these sts onto a stitch holder. Return to sts on spare needle and with RS facing rejoin yarn to next st.

Next row. K88 [95:95], turn, leaving remaining sts on a spare needle.

Continue on these sts for back.

Work 2nd-4th rows of lace pattern, now work 1st-4th rows 4 times more.

Next row. (K2 tog) 8 [13:4] times, (K1, K2 tog) 23 [22:28] times, K to end. (57 [60:63] sts). Break yarn and sl these sts onto a stitch holder.

Return to sts on spare needle and with RS of work facing rejoin yarn to next st. Continue on remaining 44 [46:46] sts for left front.

Work 1st-4th rows of lace pattern 5 times.

Next row. (K3, (K1, K2 tog) 7 [9:13] times, K2 tog 10 [8:2] times. (27 [29:31] sts)

Sl these sts onto a stitch holder for yoke.

SLEEVES
With B, cast on 55 [55:66] sts. K 3 rows.

Change to A and work 56 [60:64] rows in lace pattern as given for back and fronts. Mark each end of last row with a coloured thread.

Continue in lace pattern for 20 rows.

1st size only
Next row. (K1, K2 tog) 17 times, K to end.

2nd size only
Next row. (K1, K2 tog) 9 times, (K2, K2 tog) 6 times, K to end.

3rd size only
Next row. (K2 tog) 9 times, (K1, K2 tog) 15 times, K to end.

All sizes
Sl remaining 38 [40:42] sts onto a stitch holder.

YOKE
With B and with RS of work facing, pick up and K27 [29:31] sts from right front, then 38 [40:42] sts from first sleeve, then 57 [60:63] sts from back, then 38 [40:42] sts from second sleeve and 27 [29:31] sts from left front. (187 [198:209] sts)

Next row. K.

Shape yoke
Continue in g st stripes (every row K), working 2 rows in A, then 2 rows in B alternately, at the same time shape yoke as follows:

1st row
1st size. (K9, K2 tog) 17 times. (170 sts)

2nd size. (K7, K2 tog) 12 times, (K8, K2 tog) 8 times. K to end. (178 sts)

3rd size. K7, K2 tog, (K8, K2 tog) 19 times, K to end. (189 sts)

All sizes. Continue in g st stripes for 3 rows.

5th row
1st size. (K7, K2 tog) 9 times, (K8, K2 tog) 8 times, K to end. (153 sts)

2nd size. (K7, K2 tog) 12 times, (K8, K2 tog) 6 times, K to end. (160 sts)

3rd size. (K7, K2 tog) 11 times, (K8, K2 tog) 8 times, K to end. (170 sts)

All sizes. Continue in g st stripes for 3 rows.

9th row
1st size. (K6, K2 tog) 9 times, (K7, K2 tog) 8 times, K to end. (136 sts)

2nd size. (K6, K2 tog) 11 times, (K7, K2 tog) 7 times, K to end. (142 sts)

3rd size. (K6, K2 tog) 10 times, (K7, K2 tog) 9 times, K to end. (151 sts)

All sizes. Continue in g st stripes for 3 rows.

13th row
1st size. (K5, K2 tog) 8 times, (K6, K2 tog) 9 times, K to end. (119 sts)

2nd size. (K5, K2 tog) 10 times, (K6, K2 tog) 8 times, K to end. (124 sts)

3rd size. (K5, K2 tog) 9 times, (K6, K2 tog) 10 times, K to end. (132 sts)

All sizes. Continue in g st stripes for 3 rows.

17th row
1st size. (K4, K2 tog) 7 times, (K5, K2 tog) 10 times, K to end. (102 sts)

2nd size. (K4, K2 tog) 9 times, (K5, K2 tog) 9 times, K to end. (106 sts)

3rd size. (K4, K2 tog) 8 times, (K5, K2 tog) 11 times, K to end. (113 sts)

All sizes. Continue in g st stripes for 3 rows.

21st row
1st size. (K4, K2 tog) 10 times, (K5, K2 tog) 5 times, K to end. (87 sts)

2nd size. (K4, K2 tog) 13 times, (K5, K2 tog) 3 times, K to end. (90 sts)

3rd size. K3, K2 tog, (K4, K2 tog) 17 times, K to end. (95 sts)

All sizes. Continue in g st stripes for 3 rows.

25th row
1st size. (K3, K2 tog) 9 times, (K4, K2 tog) 6 times, K to end. (72 sts)

2nd size. (K3, K2 tog) 12 times, (K4, K2 tog) 4 times, K to end. (74 sts)

3rd size. (K3, K2 tog) 18 times, K to end. (77 sts)

All sizes. Continue in g st stripes for 3 rows.

29th row
1st size. (K2, K2 tog) 3 times, (K3, K2 tog) 11 times, K to end. (58 sts)

2nd size. K2, K2 tog, (K3, K2 tog) 13 times, K to end. (60 sts)

3rd size. (K2, K2 tog) 3 times, (K3, K2 tog) 12 times, K to end. (62 sts)

All sizes. Continue in g st stripes for 1 row.

Cast off.

BUTTON BAND

With B, cast on 6 sts. Work in g st until band, when slightly stretched, fits up front opening to top of yoke. Cast off.

BUTTONHOLE BAND

Work as given for button band but working four buttonholes, the first to come level with start of yoke, the last to come ½ cm (¼ in) below neck edge with the other two spaced evenly between them. Make buttonholes on RS rows as follows:
Buttonhole row. K2, yfwd, K2 tog, K2.

MAKING UP

Join sleeve seams up to markers using flat seams for g st sections and backstitch seams for remainder. Join rest of sleeves to front and back.

Sew on button and buttonhole bands. Sew on buttons.

Baby Coat (page 62)

If you find the lacy baby jacket a little daunting, try this simpler version in stocking stitch with a garter stitch hem and square striped yoke.

MEASUREMENTS

Age: 6 months [12 months:18 months]
To fit chest: 46 cm (18 in) [50 cm (20 in):51 cm (21½ in)]
Length to shoulder: 28 cm (11 in) [30 cm (11¾ in):32 cm (12½ in)]
Sleeve seam: 15 cm (6 in) [16 cm (6½ in):18 cm (7 in)]
Instructions are given for the smallest size first with larger sizes in the following square bracket.

MATERIALS

125 g (5 oz) [125 g (5 oz):150 g (6 oz)] 4-ply superwash wool in main colour (A)
50 g (2 oz) in contrast colour (B)
1 pair each of 2¾ mm (no 1) and 3 mm (no 2) knitting needles
4 small buttons

TENSION

30 sts and 42 rows to 10 cm (4 in) over st st on 3 mm (no 2) needles

BACK AND FRONTS
(one piece)

With 2¾ mm (no 1) needles and B, cast on 176 [182:188] sts.
K 3 rows.
Change to 3 mm (no 2) needles and A. Beg with a K row, continue in st st until work measures 17 cm (6¾ in) [18 cm (7 in):19 cm (7½ in)], ending with a P row.
Decrease for yoke
Next row. (K2, K2 tog) 39 [33:27] times, (K3, K2 tog) 3 [9:15] times, K to end. (134 [140:146] sts.)
Next row. P.
Change to B, work yoke in g st in stripes of 4 rows B, 4 rows A.
Divide for armholes
Next row. K35 [36:38] sts, turn, leaving remaining sts on a spare needle.
Continue on these sts for right front.

Shape armhole
Next row. Cast off 6 sts, K to end.
Next row. K.
**Now dec 1 st at beg of next and every alt row 3 [3:4] times. (26 [27:28] sts.)
K 31 [35:37] rows.
Shape neck
Next row. K24 [25:26] sts, turn, leaving remaining 2 sts on a safety pin.
Next row. Cast off 2 sts, K to end.
Now dec 1 st at neck edge on every row until 17 [19:19] sts remain.
K 1 [2:1] rows.
Shape shoulder
Cast off 6 sts at beg of next and following alt row.
Cast off remaining 5 [7:7] sts.
Return to sts on spare needle.
With RS of work facing, rejoin B to next st.
Next row. K70 [74:76] sts, turn, leaving remaining sts on spare needle.
Continue on these sts only for back, working in stripes as given for front.
Shape armholes
Cast off 6 sts at beg of next row.
Work 1 row. Now dec 1 st at each end of next and 2 [2:3] following alt rows. (58 [62:62] sts.)
K 39 [43:45] rows, ending with RS facing.
Shape shoulder
Cast off 6 sts at beg of next 4 rows and 5 [7:7] sts at beg of following 2 rows. Cast off the remaining 24 sts.
Return to sts on spare needle. With RS of work facing rejoin yarn to next st.
K 4 rows.
Complete to match right front, working from ** to end.

SLEEVES

With 2¾ mm (no 1) needles and B, cast on 54 [56:60] sts.
K 3 rows.
Change to 3 mm (no 2) needles and A. Continue in st st until work measures 15 cm (6 in) [16 cm (6½ in):18 cm (7 in)], ending with a P row.
Shape top
Cast off 3 sts at beg of next 2 rows. Work 2 rows.
Now dec 1 st at each end of next row.
Work 1 [3:1] rows.
Now dec 1 st at each end of next and every following alt row until 10 sts remain, ending with a P row. Cast off.

MAKING UP

Join shoulder seams.
Join sleeve seams, set in sleeves.
Neckband
With RS of work facing, with 2¾ mm (no 1) needles and B, K2 sts from right front, pick up and K12 sts up right side of neck, pick up and K28 sts from back neck and 12 sts down left side of neck, K2 sts from left front. (56 sts.)
Work in g st for 2 cm (¾ in).
Cast off loosely.
Button band
With 2¾ mm (no 1) needles and B, cast on 6 sts.
Work in g st until band when slightly stretched fits up front opening to top of yoke.
Cast off.
Buttonhole band
Work as given for button band but working four buttonholes, the first to come level with start of yoke, the last to come ½ cm (¼ in) below neck edge with the other two spaced evenly between them.
Make buttonholes on RS rows as follows:
Buttonhole row. K2, yfwd, K2 tog, K2.
Sew on button and buttonhole bands and buttons.

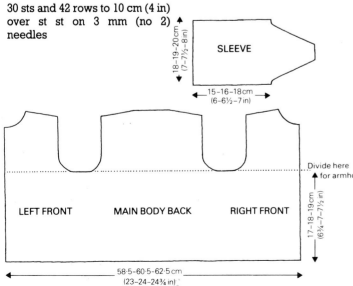

SLEEVE

18-19-20 cm (7-7½-8 in)

15-16-18 cm (6-6½-7 in)

Divide here for armhole

17-18-19 cm (6¾-7-7½ in)

LEFT FRONT   MAIN BODY BACK   RIGHT FRONT

58·5-60·5-62·5 cm (23-24-24¾ in)

FAIR ISLE ACCESSORIES

Fair Isle Accessories (page 66)

These colourful accessories consist of a pair of mittens, a pull-on hat and tube socks, which are socks worked in the round without a heel. All of them are decorated with stripes, contrast ribs and a Fair Isle pattern worked from a simple chart. For an even easier version, ignore the chart and work them entirely in stripes.

MEASUREMENTS
Age: 3 [4:5] years
Width at top of sock: 16 cm (6½ in) [17 cm (7 in):17 cm (7 in)]
Round head for cap: 44 cm (17½ in)
Round hand for mittens: 14 cm (5½ in)
Instructions are given for the smallest size first with larger sizes in the following square brackets.

MATERIALS
Socks
50 g (2 oz) superwash double knitting wool in main colour (A)
25 g (1 oz) in each of 3 contrast colours (B, C, D)

Mittens
25 g (1 oz) in each of 4 colours (A, B, C, D)

Cap
50 g (2 oz) in 1 colour (A)
25 g (1 oz) in each of 3 colours (B, C, D)

Whole set
75 g (3 oz) in 1 colour (A)
50 g (2 oz) in 1 colour (B)
25 g (1 oz) in each of 2 colours (C, D)
1 pair each of 3¼ mm (no 3) and 4 mm (no 5) knitting needles
1 set each of 4 double-pointed 3¼ mm (no 3) and 4 mm (no 5) knitting needles (for socks)

TENSION
22 sts and 28 rows to 10 cm (4 in) over st st on 4 mm (no 5) needles

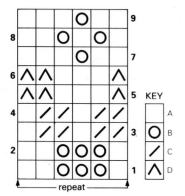

CAP
With 3¼ mm (no 3) needles and B, cast on 98 sts. Work in K1, P1 rib for 2 cm (¾ in).
Change to 4 mm (no 5) needles and C. Work 6 rows st st beg with a K row. Continue in st st, work 2 rows in A, then 2 rows in D. Now work Fair Isle pattern from chart as follows:
1st row. K1A, *1A, 3B, 2A; repeat from * to last st, K1A.
2nd row. P1A, *2A, 3B, 1A; repeat from * to last st, P1A.
These 2 rows set the pattern. Continue working 3rd-9th rows from chart reading K rows from right to left and P rows from left to right, and working edge sts in A as set.
Continue in st st, work 1 row in A, then 2 rows in D. Now with A only, work straight until cap measures 12 cm (5 in).
Shape crown
1st row. (K4, K2 tog) 8 times, (K3, K2 tog) 10 times. (80 sts)
2nd and every alt row. P.
3rd row. (K2 tog, K2) to end of row. (60 sts)
5th row. (K2 tog, K1) to end of row. (40 sts)
7th row. (K2 tog) to end. (20 sts)
9th row. (K2 tog) to end. (10 sts)
Break yarn and thread through remaining sts. Draw up and fasten off securely.

SOCKS (both alike)
With set of four double-pointed 3¼ mm (no 3) needles and B, cast on 36 [40:40] sts. Divide sts between three needles using fourth needle to work in rounds. Work in K2, P2 rib, working 6 rows in B, 2 rows in A, 2 rows in C, 2 rows in D. Now work 4 rows in B inc 2 sts evenly across last row on 2nd and 3rd sizes only. (36 [42:42] sts)
Change to 4 mm (no 5) needles and C, work 6 rows in st st (K every round).
Continue in st st, work 2 rounds in A, then 2 rounds in D. Now work Fair Isle pattern from chart as follows:
1st round. *K1A, 3B, 2A; repeat

from * to end of round.
2nd round. As 1st round.
These 2 rounds set the pattern. Continue working 3rd-9th rounds from chart reading every row on chart from right to left. Continue in st st, work 1 round in A, then 2 rounds in D. With A only work straight until sock measures 25 cm (10 in).
Change to B. Now shape toe as follows:
2nd and 3rd sizes only
Next round. (K5, K2 tog) 6 times. (36 sts)
Next round. K.
All sizes
1st round. (K4, K2 tog) 6 times. (30 sts)
2nd and every alt round. K.
3rd round. (K3, K2 tog) 6 times. (24 sts)
5th round. (K2, K2 tog) 6 times. (18 sts)
7th round. (K1, K2 tog) 6 times. (12 sts)
9th round. (K2 tog) 6 times. (6 sts)
Break yarn and thread through remaining sts. Draw up and fasten off securely.

RIGHT-HAND MITTEN
With 3¼ mm (no 3) needles and B, cast on 30 sts. Work in K1, P1 rib for 5 cm (2 in).
Change to 4 mm (no 5) needles and A.
Continue in st st, work 2 rows.
Shape thumb gusset
1st row. K15, inc 1 into next st, K1, inc 1 into next st, K12.
2nd-4th rows. Work in st st.
5th row. K15, inc 1 into next st, K3, inc 1 into next st, K12.
Continue in this way, inc 1 st on each side of gusset on every 4th row until there are 38 sts on needle.
Next row. P.
Next row. K27, turn and cast on 2 sts.
Next row. P12, turn and cast on 2 sts.
Continue on these 14 sts for 2.5 cm (1 in) ending with a P row.
Next row. (K2 tog) to end. (7 sts)
Break yarn and thread through remaining sts. Draw up and fasten off securely. Join thumb seam.
With RH needle pick up and K4 sts from base of thumb, K to end of row. (32 sts)
Next row. P.
Continue in st st, work 2 rows in

colour D.
Now work 1st-9th rows in Fair Isle pattern from chart as given for cap.
Continue in st st, work 1 row in A, then 2 rows in D.
Change to A.
Shape top
1st row. K1, K2 tog, K11, K2 tog, K1, K2 tog, K10, K2 tog, K1.
2nd and every alt row. P.
3rd row. K1, K2 tog, K9, K2 tog, K1, K2 tog, K8, K2 tog, K1.
5th row. K1, K2 tog, K7, K2 tog, K1, K2 tog, K6, K2 tog, K1.
6th row. P.
Cast off.

LEFT-HAND MITTEN
Work as given for right-hand mitten reversing shaping for thumb gusset as follows:
1st row. K12, inc 1 into next st, K1, inc 1 into next st, K15.
2nd-4th rows. Work in st st.
Continue in this way inc 1 st on each side of gusset on every 4th row until there are 38 sts.
Next row. P.
Next row. K21, turn and cast on 2 sts.
Next row. P12, turn and cast on 2 sts. (14 sts)
Complete as given for right-hand mitten.

MAKING UP
Press all pieces according to instructions on ball band. Join back seam on cap and mitten seams invisibly.
Thread shirring elastic through sock tops if required.

Pegbag

MATERIALS

100 g (4 oz) double knitting wool in main colour (A)
50 g (2 oz) in blue (B)
Oddments in 3 shades of green (C, D, E), brown (F) and any 3 other contrast colours
1 pair 4 mm (no 5) knitting needles
1 cable needle
2 30 cm (12 in) long pieces of bamboo garden cane

FRONT

With B, cast on 52 sts. Work 92 rows in st st. Continue in st st, work 18 rows in A. Cast off.

BACK

With A, cast on 52 sts. Work 92 rows in st st. Continue in st st, work 18 rows in D. Cast off.

HEDGE

With E, cast on 50 sts. Work in moss st as follows:
1st row. (K1, P1) to end.
2nd row. (P1, K1) to end.
Repeat these 2 rows 5 times more. Change to C and work 4 rows in K1, P1 rib. Cast off.

TREE TRUNK

With F, cast on 7 sts. Work in mock rib as follows:
1st row. (WS) K1, *P1, K1; repeat from * to end.
2nd row. P1, *sl 1 with yarn on RS, P1; repeat from * to end.
Repeat these 2 rows 23 times more. Cast off.

TREE TOP

With D, cast on 13 sts. Commence cluster pattern working from chart below. Work 2 rows in st st, beg with a K row.
Next row. K1, *K next 3 sts then sl them onto cable needle and wind E 6 times clockwise round these sts, beg and ending with E at back of work, sl sts from cable needle back on to RH needle, K1; repeat from * to end. Break off E.

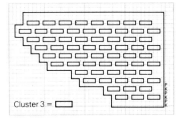

Cluster 3 = ▭

Next row. Cast on 2 sts, P to end. Continue in this way working from chart, shaping and clustering groups of 3 sts as before where shown.

PLAIN JUMPER

With any colour, cast on 8 sts.
1st row. (K1, tbl, P1 tbl) to end.
2nd row. (K1, P1) to end.
3rd-8th rows. Work in st st.
9th row. Cast on 4 sts, K to end. (12 sts)
10th row. Cast on 4 sts, P to end. (16 sts)
11th-18th rows. Work in st st.
19th row. Cast off 4 sts, K to end.
20th row. Cast off 4 sts, P to end. (8 sts)
Work 6 rows in st st, then 2 rows in K1, P1 rib. Cast off.

STRIPED JUMPER
Body

Using any colour, cast on 16 sts.* Work 2 rows g st. With contrast yarns work 2-row g st stripes for 4 rows. Repeat from * once, then work 2 more rows in first colour.
Cast off.

Sleeves

Cast on 6 sts, work as given for body until 10 rows have been worked.
Cast off.

Front border

With A, cast on 192 sts loosely. Work 8 rows in g st. Cast off.

Handles (make 2)

With A, cast on 14 sts. Work 150 rows in st st (approx 50 cm/20 in). Cast off.

Facing (make 2)

With A, cast on 40 sts. Work 8 rows in g st. Cast off.

MAKING UP

Pin out back and front of bag. Turn over contrast colour casings for handles, using reverse side of st st for RS of picture. Press lightly over a damp cloth. Press all other pieces worked in st st.
Sew handle casings in place. Join short ends of border and pin it out to frame picture with cast-off edge on outside. Sew frame in place.
Arrange picture inside border. Sew down tree trunk and tree top. Place hedge in position easing rib base to fit and pulling up top into rounded shapes. Sew hedge in place. Sew up jumpers. Make a twisted cord about 20 cm (8 in) long for washing line and lay it across picture, tucking ends behind tree trunk and border. Sew jumpers on at shoulders with straight stitches to resemble pegs.
Sew back and front of bag together leaving about 8 cm (3 in) open each side below handles. Sew facing to inside top of bag below handles on each side.
Fold handles in half lengthwise and join long sides together. Insert bamboo into slots. Join handles firmly round each end of bamboo.
Make two tassels with oddments and sew below handles on each side of bag front.

ALLSORTS
PICTURE CUSHIONS

Allsorts (page 70)

MATERIALS
Black and orange cube
100 g (4 oz) chunky yarn in black (A)
50 g (2 oz) in orange (B)
Yellow and black cube
200 g (8 oz) in yellow (C)
50 g (2 oz) in black (A)
Black and white allsort
100 g (4 oz) in black (A)
50 g (2 oz) in white (D)
Black and white round allsort
100 g (4 oz) in black (A)
50 g (2 oz) in white (D)
Pink and black allsort
200 g (8 oz) in pink (E)
50 g (2 oz) in black (A)
Whole set
350 g (14 oz) in black
50 g (2 oz) white
200 g (8 oz) in pink
50 g (2 oz) in orange
200 g (7 oz) in yellow
1 pair 7 mm (no 10½) needles
Stuffing (solid foam or chippings)

BLACK AND ORANGE CUBE
Side pieces (make 4)
With A, cast on 22 sts.
Work in g st stripes as follows:
1st-8th rows. A.
9th-16th rows. B.
Repeat these 16 rows once more, then the first 8 rows again. Cast off.

End pieces (make 2)
With A, cast on 22 sts.
Work 40 rows in g st. Cast off.

MAKING UP
Do not press. Sew up cube leaving one seam open. Stuff and close remaining seam.

YELLOW AND BLACK CUBE
Side pieces (make 4)
With C, cast on 22 sts. Work 16 rows in g st. Continue in g st, work 8 rows in A, then 16 rows in C. Cast off.

End pieces (make 2)
With C, cast on 22 sts. Work 40 rows in g st. Cast off.

MAKING UP
Complete as given for black and orange cube.

BLACK AND WHITE ALLSORT
Side pieces (make 4)
With A, cast on 22 sts. Work 8 rows in g st. Continue in g st, work 8 rows in D, then 8 rows in A. Cast off.

End pieces (make 4)
Work as given for black and orange cube.

MAKING UP
Complete as given for black and orange cube.

BLACK AND WHITE ROUND ALLSORT
Side piece
With A, cast on 22 sts. Work 80 rows in g st. Cast off.

End pieces (make 2)
With A, cast on 6 sts. Work in g st from chart a as follows. Work 2 rows straight. Cast on 2 sts at beg and end of next row. Work 1 row.
Next row. With A, inc 1 into next st, K3, K2D, with A, K3, inc 1 into last st.
Next row. K5A, 2D, 5A.
Continue working from chart a, inc 1 st at each end of following 3rd row, then dec as shown until chart is complete.
Cast off.

MAKING UP
Darn in loose ends. Join long seam of side piece to make tube. Sew one end piece in position. Stuff with foam chippings or rolled up sheet foam. Sew on remaining end piece.

PINK AND BLACK ALLSORT
Side piece
With E, cast on 22 sts. Work 140 rows in g st. Cast off.

End pieces (make 2)
With E, cast on 8 sts. Work in g st from chart b, inc at each end of 3rd, 5th, 7th, 9th, 13th and 17th rows and joining in A on 15th row as shown. Follow chart to complete shaping. Cast off.

MAKING UP
Complete as given for previous cushion.

Picture Cushions (page 71)

MEASUREMENTS
Finished cushion 35.5 cm (14 in) square
Knitted panel 23 cm (9 in) square

MATERIALS
Sheep cushion
Oddments of 4-ply yarns in 11 colours and assorted textures (see key to chart a for details)

Cherry tree cushion
Oddments of 4-ply yarns in 10 colours and assorted textures (see key to chart b for details)
1 pair 3¼ mm (no 3) needles
40 cm (½ yd) of 140 cm (54 in) wide fine tweed fabric (for each cushion)
1.25 cm (10 in) zip (for each cushion)

TENSION
26 sts and 36 rows to 10 cm (4 in) over st st on 3¼ mm (no 3) needles

SHEEP PANEL
Cast on 58 sts.
Using colours as indicated in key follow chart a, work in st st. When 81 rows of chart have been completed cast off.

CHERRY TREE PANEL
Cast on 58 sts.
Using colours as indicated in key follow chart b, work in st st K the first and every following alt row reading from right to left, P the second and every following alt row reading from left to right. On K rows work from A to B twice, then from A to C. On P rows work from C to A, then from B to A twice. When 81 rows of chart have been completed cast off.

MAKING UP
Darn in loose ends securely. Make up both covers alike. Pin

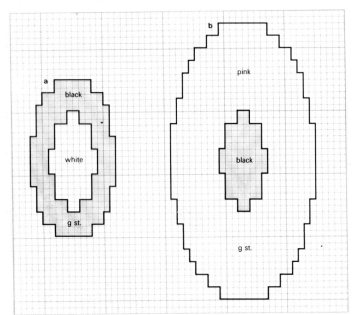

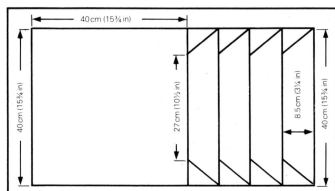

out panel to 23 cm (9 in) square. Press with warm iron over damp cloth. Textured yarns such as mohair can be raised by gentle brushing to give more depth and life to the landscape.

Cut fabric following layout. Sew borders together taking in 2 cm (¾ in) seams to make a frame as shown. Press seams open.

Position knitted panel in centre of frame and oversew joins on WS. Sew back of cushion to front taking in 2 cm (¾ in) seams leaving 25 cm (10 in) open on one side for zip. Insert zip.

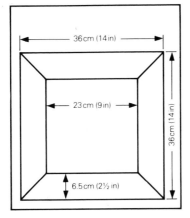

Keys to picture cushion charts

key to chart a
1 grey
2 dark brown
3 lovat green
4 light green
5 bottle green
6 mixed wool, medium green
7 mid-green
8 green mohair stripes
9 mixture, light green
10 white bouclé
11 black

key to chart b
1 grey
2 light brown bouclé
3 pink for blossoms
4 light green
5 light brown
6 turquoise/pink for flowers
7 dark brown
8 green and yellow mixed
9 green/pink bouclé mixture
10 green mohair

chart a   chart b

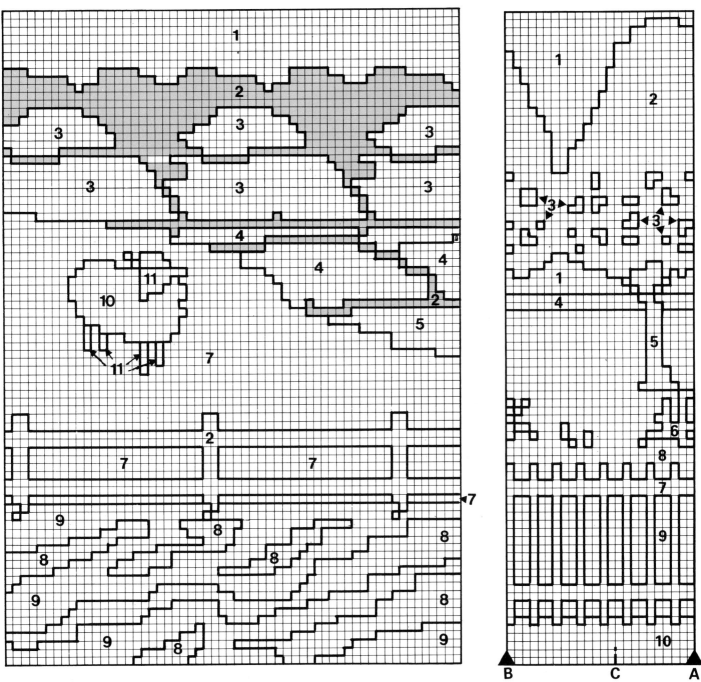

BEDSPREAD

Chart 1

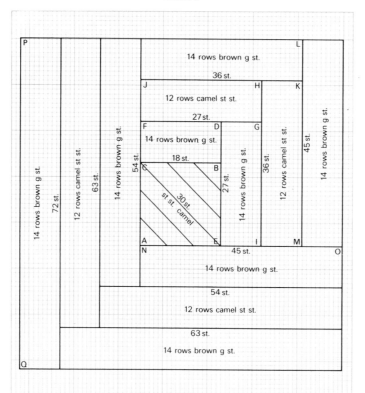

Chart 2

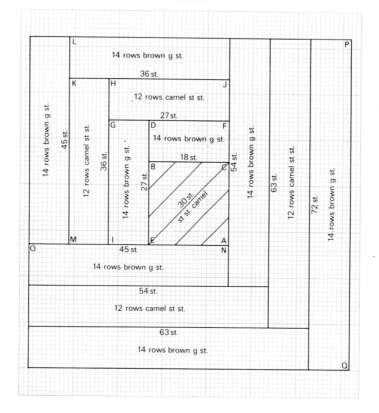

Bedspread (page 74)

MATERIALS
1350 g (54 oz) Aran weight wool in brown
1000 g (40 oz) in cream
350 g (14 oz) in camel
200 g (8 oz) in mid-green
150 g (6 oz) in dark grey
50 g (2 oz) each in dark green, light grey and ginger
1 pair 6 mm (no 9) knitting needles

DAISY STITCH
1st row. (RS) K.
2nd row. K1, *P3 tog without dropping sts off LH needle, yrn, P tog same 3 sts again, K1; repeat from * to end.
3rd row. K.
4th row. K1, P1, K1, *P3 tog without dropping sts off LH needle, yrn, P tog same 3 sts again, K1; repeat from * to last 2 sts, P1, K1.
These 4 rows form the pattern repeat.

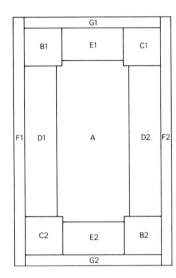

SECTION A
With brown cast on 110 sts. Work 14 rows g st (as chart 3, left and opposite). Continue working from chart 1 following instructions for shaping, colour and stitch pattern. (For ease of working transfer chart to one large sheet of graph paper.) Twist contrast yarns tog at back to avoid holes. When all 344 rows of the chart have been worked, cast off.

SECTIONS B1 AND B2
Work from chart 1 on page 74, beg at A, with camel cast on 2 sts. Continue in st st, inc 1 st at each end of every row until there are 30 sts. Now dec 1 st at each end of every row until 2 sts remain. Pass 1 st over other and pull yarn through remaining st to fasten off at B.
With RS facing and brown, pick up and K18 sts between B and C. Work 13 more rows in g st. Leave these sts on spare needle.
With RS facing and brown, pick up and K27 sts between E and D. Work 13 more rows g st. Leave these sts on spare needle.
Now return to sts on previous spare needle. With RS facing and camel, pick up and K9 sts from G to D, then K across 18 sts from D to F. (27 sts) Work 11 more rows st st. Leave these sts on spare needle.
With RS facing, return to sts on previous spare needle. With camel, K across 27 sts from I to G, then pick up and K9 sts from G to H. (36 sts). Work 11 more rows st st. Leave these sts on spare needle.
Return to sts on previous spare needle. With RS facing and brown, pick up and K9 sts from K to H then K across 27 sts from H to J. (36 sts) Work 13 more rows g st. Cast off.
Return to sts on previous spare needle. With RS facing and brown, K across 36 sts from M to K, then pick up and K9 sts from K to L. (45 sts) Work 13 more rows g st. Cast off.
Work rest of this square from chart 1, always pick up sts with RS facing and working colours and rows as indicated. Beg at N/O with brown and end at P/Q with brown.

Chart 3

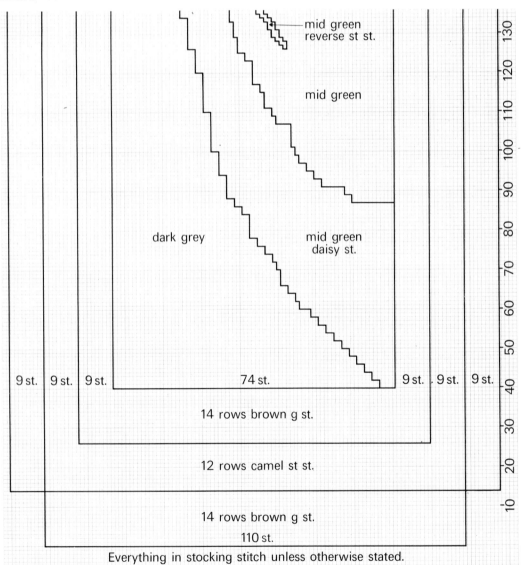

Everything in stocking stitch unless otherwise stated.
Fancy stitch instructions given previously.

Chart 3

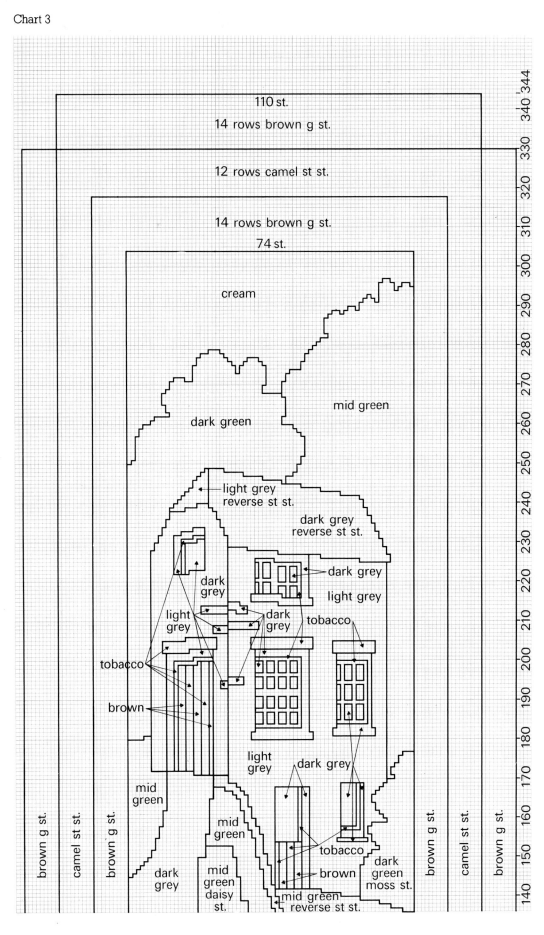

110 st.

14 rows brown g st.

344
340

330

12 rows camel st st.

320

14 rows brown g st.

310

74 st.

300

cream

290

280

mid green

270

dark green

260

250

light grey
reverse st st.

240

dark grey
reverse st st.

230

dark grey

220

dark
grey

light grey

210

light
grey

dark
grey

tobacco

200

tobacco

190

brown

180

light
grey

dark grey

170

mid
green

160

mid
green

150

mid
green

dark
grey

mid
green
daisy
st.

mid
green

tobacco

brown

dark
green
moss st.

140

mid green
reverse st st.

brown g st.

camel st st.

brown g st.

brown g st.

camel st st.

brown g st.

SECTIONS C1 AND C2
These squares are worked as a mirror image of sections B1 and B2. Work from chart 2 on page 74, beg at A and ending at P/Q.

SECTIONS D1 AND D2
With cream, cast on 63 sts. Work 316 rows st st. Cast off.

SECTIONS E1 AND E2
With cream, cast on 63 sts. Work 316 rows st st. Cast off.

SECTIONS F1 AND F2
With brown, cast on 18 sts. Work in g st until strip fits top edge. Cast off.

SECTIONS G1 AND G2
With brown, cast on 18 sts. Work in g st until strip fits side edge. Cast off.

MAKING UP
Darn in loose ends neatly.
Press all the pieces carefully avoiding g st. Join all sections together following the diagram on page 76, working from section A outwards. Press seams.

INDEX

ACKNOWLEDGMENTS

The publishers wish to thank the following organizations and individuals for their kind permission to reproduce the pictures in this book:

BBC Hulton Picture Library 8; Topham Picture Library 9; Victoria and Albert Museum 6, 7 above, 7 below

Special Photography by:

Belinda 47, 50-51; Theo Bergstrom 43; John Carter 42; Oliver Haten 2-3; Sandra Lousada 46, 54, 55, 58, 59, 62-63, 66-67; Coral Mulla 15-23, 26-29, 32-37; Spike Powell 70, 75; Charles Stebbings 14; Jerry Tubby 70-71

BACKGROUND PHOTOGRAPHY: THEO BERGSTROM
FRONT PANEL PHOTOGRAPHY: SANDRA LOUSADA
BACK PANEL PHOTOGRAPHY: CAROL SHARP